wish you were here

A COLLECTION OF ESSAYS

from the editor of *Our State* magazine

Our State

DOWN HOME IN NORTH CAROLINA

wish you were here

Published by *Our State* magazine, Greensboro, N.C.

Wish You Were Here
copyright © 2013 by *Our State* magazine.
All rights reserved.
Published by Mann Media Inc.
P.O. Box 4552, Greensboro, N.C. 27404
(800) 948-1409 | ourstate.com
Printed in the United States by R.R. Donnelley

by **ELIZABETH HUDSON**

illustrated by **SUZANNE & EDGAR CABRERA**

designed by **JASON CHENIER**

Library of Congress Control Number: 2013942097

Contents

The Start of Something

WHEN **I** BEGAN WORKING at *Our State* in 1997, my job was to answer the phone and open the mail in the circulation department.

It was my dream to work for the magazine, and although I aspired to be in the editorial department, if I'd been hired to sweep the floors, I'd have been just as happy.

Back then, if you called to renew a subscription, you probably talked to me. If you mailed a letter, I probably opened it. And if you put a special stamp on that letter, then you probably made my day.

playwright and author of *Our Town,* posing with his hands folded beneath his chin, a village with a small, white church in the background.

The stamp cost 32 cents, and it was beautiful, a miniature work of art.

I have no idea why that particular stamp struck me — maybe I was drawn to the way it reminded me of so many small towns in North Carolina — but I cut it away from the envelope and pinned it to my wall.

Then I started looking for more.

Commemorative stamps are larger than the one-inch-square regular-issue stamps. These stamps are special.

And then I realized, this is how collections evolve. The pleasure is in the pursuit.

Back then, we didn't have a website. We didn't have email. So the mail was important. Every day, I'd go to the post office and collect the day's mail in a big crate. Back at the office, I'd sort through it all and open it. I sat in a small room, facing a beige wall, and the task took me about four hours to complete.

One day, as I was riffling through white envelope after white envelope, I noticed an interesting stamp on a letter. It was a picture of Thornton Wilder, the Pulitzer Prize- winning

They're produced in limited quantities and intended to memorialize a person or a place, or honor an achievement or a historic event.

Within the year, I covered the wall in front of me with stamps. I got some great ones. There was the "Hollywood Legends" series: James Dean. Marilyn Monroe. Cary Grant. Alfred Hitchcock. I had the "American Music" series with Benny Goodman on his clarinet and Glenn Miller on trombone. There was the "Four Centuries of American Art"

series, with Grant Wood and Winslow Homer and Edward Hopper's *Nighthawks*.

Once, I got an Air Mail stamp. It was pink, and on it was a picture of a winged flyer and the faces of two men: The Wright Brothers. You'd have thought someone had sent me a $100 bill.

A "Great Lakes Lighthouses" series, with lighthouses from Lake Erie and Lake Superior, made me think that Cape Hatteras was surely deserving of its own stamp. Then I found out that the United States Post Office thought so, too. That stamp was created in 1972.

I wanted to find it.

And then I realized, this is how collections evolve. The pleasure is in the pursuit.

I miss the mail sometimes.

I still have all those stamps, stored, appropriately, in an envelope. I can't bring myself to throw them away. They remind me of where I started at *Our State,* and they remind me that no matter how much things change, it's important to have something to look forward to, something to set your sights toward. I never did get that Cape Hatteras stamp, but maybe I'll run across it one day at an auction or an antiques festival. I'll keep my eyes open.

Because that's the beautiful thing about finding something you connect with, no matter how small it is. It lets you become a collector of memories and a keeper of dreams.

The Long Way Home

I REMEMBER THE SUMMER my dad came home with his new truck, a red pickup.

We had just moved from town, from a house that was right behind the courthouse in Asheboro, to the country, to a house that was right in front of a dirt road, and my dad believed that a man living in the country should have a truck.

He was proud of that truck. And I was, too. We took it all over town, my dad and me, riding high in the cab with the windows rolled down, hot breezes blowing across the dashboard.

On the nights when my mom worked late at her shop, my dad and I would ride to town to pick up dinner.

When I was a kid, Asheboro had plenty of family-style, sit-down restaurants, but I don't remember too many options for a quick take-out meal.

There was Rays. There was Hardee's. And there was McDonald's.

From our house heading back to town, McDonald's was the first fast-food restaurant you came to.

For the next 20 years, my dad drove everywhere in that truck.

We always went through the drive-through, presumably so that we wouldn't have to get out of the truck at all, kicking off a ritual that my dad and I would enact many times over the years, until I was finally old enough to drive, and I became too much of a teenager to ride with him anymore.

At McDonald's, Dad would lean in toward the speakers, and in his deep, clear voice, he'd order the same thing for both of us every time: Two double cheeseburgers. Two small fries. Two small Cokes. Then we'd take the long way home. I'd stare into the night as Dad drove, a warm McDonald's bag on my lap, the glow of the AM/FM radio on the console. For the next 20 years, my dad drove everywhere in that truck. He hauled me all over town, shuttling me to school in the fall and to my grandmother's house in the summer.

He hauled the inventory from my mom's store the year she moved it from downtown to the mall. Years later, when business got so bad my mom had to close her store, my dad loaded up the truck bed, scarred now from years of use, with the old cash registers and the long, wooden display tables that once held pounds of cross-stitch fabric and picture frames.

He hauled peaches and watermelons from Candor in the back of that truck. He hauled mulch for the yard and Christmas trees for our living room. When I went off to college, he hauled everything I took for my dorm room.

In the summertime, he hauled my friends and me. We climbed in the back of the truck bed and went wherever he was going, just for the chance to ride in the open air, watching everything we passed get smaller in the distance.

When I got too old to ride with him, he hauled my dog, a short-legged feist-dachshund named Muffin.

Muffin loved riding in the truck even more than I did. If my dad walked to the truck, Muffin ran to stand beside it. She was too short to jump in, and I can remember watching my dad, on those evenings when I had my own places to go, reach down to scoop her up and set her on the seat. She kept him from having to ride alone.

A few years ago, my dad sold the truck. It had 350,000 miles on it, and it started to have some problems. My dad no longer had as much to haul around, so he relegated the truck to a spot at the end of the property, where it sat for a long time.

Evidently, someone noticed it.

One day, my dad was working in the yard when a 16-year-old kid and his dad pulled up.

"Your truck for sale?" the kid called out across the yard. He was polite. And hopeful.

My dad looked at him for a long while and finally told the kid, "I'll take $300 for it."

The kid looked at his dad and said, "I'll be right back."

They came back in about an hour, cash in hand. They got in the truck, the kid and his dad, and drove off.

My dad watched the truck go down the road for as long as he could, until he finally had to turn away.

A Good Year for Peaches

EFORE I CAME ALONG, and before my parents opened their small business and got busy with the routine of building a life and a home, they were just two people in love.

Their first date was at a pizza place in High Point. My mom, who grew up poor and in the country, had never eaten pizza before, and she was so excited. My dad was charmed by her enthusiasm for everything, and after that, he wanted to take her everywhere.

They packed picnics and spent Sunday afternoons at High Point Lake. They went to Calabash and ate fried flounder and watched the sun set over the water. They took my dad's Buick Skylark to the Blue Ridge Parkway, the two of them sitting side by side.

At night, they got dressed up — I've seen photos of my mom in a plaid, sleeveless dress, her hair teased sky-high, and my dad in a suit coat, his thick, black hair slicked down — and they went to fancier places like the Zevely House in Winston-Salem; Cellar Antons in Greensboro, which they knew as Irving Park Delicatessen; and Le Chateau in High Point.

Once, my parents drove all the way to Myrtle Beach, so my dad could take my mom to a Chinese restaurant he knew about there. She ordered Moo Goo Gai Pan and liked it so much that she talked about it for years.

At The Peddler in High Point, where the servers cut your steaks by candlelight at the table, my dad gave my mom a diamond ring.

I can only imagine how happy the two of them must have looked then.

Eventually, over the years, they stayed in more than they went out. The demands of running a business and raising a family meant they stopped going out to eat so much. They didn't take any trips.

And then one day, a few years ago, I came home from work and found, on my doorstep, a white cardboard box with a quart of peaches from Johnson's Peach Outlet in Candor.

There was an index card sticking up from the box, and in my mom's handwriting, it said: July 23 — Mom and Dad went to peach orchard and cruised through Seagrove. Fun Sunday afternoon.

On the back of the note, she had written out the recipe for her old-

Susie Hudson's Peach Cobbler

1 cup milk

1 cup sugar

1 cup self-rising flour

1 stick butter

1 quart fresh peach slices

Mix together milk, sugar, and flour. Melt butter in the bottom of a baking pan. Add peaches. Slowly pour flour mixture on top of peaches. Bake at 400° for 45 minutes or until golden brown.

fashioned peach cobbler, something that she made for my dad years ago, a simple dish with ingredients she knew.

I smiled immediately, imagining the two of them taking a summer afternoon drive out into the countryside, the way they used to. I could picture the two of them together, my mom's excitement over bringing home a new piece of pottery and a basket of peaches and maybe a few ears of sweet corn. I could imagine my dad, casually leaning against the car as he watched her, amused and admiring, the same way he did more than 40 years ago.

I made a peach cobbler myself that night, and I could taste my parents' day — sweet, simple, and tender — in every bite.

The Stars at Night

THE FIRE TOWER AT THE TOP OF DAVE'S MOUNTAIN in Asheboro is 100 feet tall, and it was built in 1950, and I wonder how many teenage boys — how many Asheboro High School kids in 1954, say, or 1967 or 1975 — drove up here and parked their cars, their Pontiacs, say, or their Skylarks or their Chevelles, and climbed the scaffolding, dungarees rolled up or cigarettes clamped between lips or long hair tucked behind their ears. I wonder how many kids, too nervous to break the rules and scramble up the girders, instead lay on the hoods of their cars, heads back against the windshields, car windows rolled down and music drifting out, Eddie Fisher, say, or Procol Harum or the Marshall Tucker Band, and stared up at the dark, night sky, up here 1,000 feet above the rest of the town, nothing in view but a million, tiny, glistening stars.

My dad climbed this tower when he was in high school in the early '50s. He was a Scout, and to earn one of his merit badges, he had to observe a forest ranger at the top of the tower for a week. Subdivisions hadn't been built on the slopes of the mountain yet, and the road wasn't paved. Every afternoon, he drove his '48 Chevy up the dirt road, parked at the bottom of the tower, and climbed the stairs to get to the trap door at the top.

My dad wedged into the tight space next to a ranger, who sat on a small, four-legged stool with its legs screwed into glass insulators, and the two of them scanned the landscape below for a hint of anything lit — a match, a flame, some spark or ember.

The unobstructed view, high above the treetops, was surely something to see — a panorama of the surrounding Uwharries; a small town made even smaller by the shift in perspective.

> "All you could think is where'd all these stars come from?"

By early evening, the lights of the town started to pop out, and the sky above faded to blue then purple then shades of black and finally disappeared altogether.

They were supposed to keep an eye out, of course, for fire in the trees below, something likely started by a stray bolt of lightning, and I'm sure the ranger kept up his end of the job. But when night fell, my dad couldn't stop looking up.

Even now, when he talks of this, I can sense the awe coming back to him, the memory of what it felt like to be up here. So far from the ground. So close to the sky.

"All you could think," he says, slowly shaking his head, "is where'd all these stars come from?"

As if he was asking how something so invisible could suddenly become so clear.

I never climbed the Asheboro fire tower, but not too long ago, I did climb the tower in Montgomery County. A ranger with the Uwharrie National Forest took me up, and it was a dizzying, nerve-racking climb in broad daylight. I can't imagine how frightening — or maybe exhilarating — it would be to climb this thing at night.

When we got to the top, I saw that someone named Andy had been here also — he had scratched his name, along with a girl's name, into the metal crossbars — and I'm willing to bet Andy and his girl weren't here in the daytime.

I'm willing to bet that Andy and his girl snuck in at night, the way people have been doing for generations, and made the climb to the top, two people staring out at nothing and everything at the same time, into the pitch-black darkness, and looking toward the sky. Because that's where the light is.

Season of Plenty

THE TOMATOES HAVE FINALLY **COME IN.** They're spread out all over the old wooden tables at the Greensboro Farmers Curb Market. Piled up in crates behind the tables. Clustered in bags beneath the tables. There are the Better Boys and Big Beefs; the Romas and Cherokee Purples; the Brandywine Pinks and Mr. Stripeys.

But everybody is looking for the German Johnsons.

Each ten-foot table is filled with something: tomatoes, of course, but also cucumbers and lettuce and 'silver queen' corn and white potatoes spilling from wooden peck-and-bushel baskets. Blackberries and scuppernongs and peaches and piles of pole beans and green beans and snap beans and string beans, depending on what you call them. Cantaloupes and watermelons. There are herb plants speared with plastic picks and identified by scrawled Sharpie

This is summertime in North Carolina.

By 7 a.m., this place is filled with people. There are the older men who wear Carolina Farm Credit caps and tan Members Only jackets to cover their overalls. They bring their wives, the older women who wear plastic Food Lion bags filled with cucumbers and squash around their wrists. By 10 a.m., the young couples who wear baby slings come. The crowd changes, but everyone leans over those old tomato tables the same way, and it's the same motion every time: fingertips grip the crown like the machine at a carnival — insert a quarter, and a metal claw picks the prize. The men and the women and the young couples dig dollar bills out of their pockets, and they move on. There are 82 more tables to get to.

lettering on yellowing index cards: basil ($3) and rosemary ($3) and lemon verbena ($4) and butterfly bush ($5).

Tables hold jars of chow-chow and half-pound cakes and homemade buttermilk pies with Saran Wrap stretched across the top like slick skin. There are eggs and meat and breads and muffins. And there are plenty of flowers.

At the end of an aisle, four of those 10-foot tables hold galvanized buckets that hold lisianthus and irises and Shasta daisies and red geraniums. The flower vendor has been here since 1973; her mother is 86, and she's here, too, tying stalks of dried hydrangeas. The mother sits in a tall chair and has her feet planted on a red-slatted footstool. She touches the forearm of everyone who stops to talk, and she offers advice to a customer who's buying a tall cut-flower arrangement for a centerpiece. "Are you sitting down at the table to eat?" she asks. "Then let's cut these shorter." She reaches for a pair of pink Fiskars cutters and lets the severed stems fall to the floor.

The floor is remarkably clean, and everyone in this building keeps his space neat and tidy. Behind most of the tables are large Igloo coolers that transported the tomatoes and the corn and the cantaloupes, the pies and breads, the cheeses and the bacon and the eggs and the flowers this morning from farms in Gibsonville and McLeansville and Reidsville and Madison. Half-eaten biscuits from Biscuitville, still loosely wrapped in yellow wax paper, sit on top of nearly everyone's coolers. Beneath one table, two quarts of blackberries sit, squirreled away for later.

On another table, a vendor keeps money in a worn Tampa Nugget cigar box. She covers the box in a pink towel and smooths a plastic bag over top of it, a homemade security system. Nobody bothers it. She opens and closes the box 40 times in an hour, trading change for all those tomatoes — the Better Boys, the Big Beefs, the Brandywine Pinks, and the one everyone wants, the German Johnsons — that she hauled to market today. She works hard, and by the end of the day, you hope that her table is empty. You hope that her box is full.

This is summertime in North Carolina — our season of abundance, when the days are the longest, the earth yields its full capacity, and tables all across the state are filled with everything anyone could ever want.

A Handmade Christmas

I**N 1982, MY MOTHER STARTED TYING BOWS** to sell in her crafts shop. Back then, there weren't any big-box arts and crafts shops; no Michaels or Hobby Lobbys. There wasn't even a Walmart.

People came in to her store every day, asking for bows to put on their mailboxes and fences. They hung bows on grapevine wreaths and bedposts; they ran bows up staircase banisters. Bows were an inexpensive decoration for a lot of households in rural North Carolina. Even men came in to the store to buy bows for the fronts of their cars.

To keep up with this demand, my mother tied bows every night. This is what I remember: After she closed her shop for the evening and came home, she kept working. She ate a warmed-up dinner plate of food, and then she gathered an armload of red velvet ribbon in 25-yard spools, stacking the spools next to her chair in the den. Most nights, I sat on the floor next to her and did my homework, and I remember hearing the soft whoosh as she tugged on a spool, uncurling five yards of ribbon at a time. She tied bows until about 11 p.m. every night, piling up a hill of them on the floor to take to work the next day.

My dad made bow boards out of 4-by-8-foot sheets of plywood Peg-Board and propped them against the walls in the shop. My mom sold her bows as fast as she could make them, as fast as she could pin them to that bow board. She sold about 100 bows a day, but at Christmastime, she sold a lot more. 500 bows. 700 bows. All in one day. It's hard to imagine.

She kept this up for another eight years, until she closed her shop 22 years ago.

I remembered all of this when we decided to put a bow on the cover of our annual Christmas issue, and it seemed fitting that I ask my mother if she'd be willing to tie a bow we could photograph.

After a few minutes of watching, I stopped seeing the bow at all. I started to notice her hands.

I bought a roll of red velvet, took it to my parents' house, and watched my mother go to work. I watched her go through the familiar steps: unfurl, cut, gather, twist, and pull the loops. She tied a few to get the right one, and after a few minutes of watching, I stopped seeing the bow at all. I started to notice her hands.

My mother's hands have seen a lot of work. They've tied a lot of bows, but before that, they strung tobacco and they picked peas. They scrubbed floors and they turned beet-red in hot dishwater and they held paintbrushes and hammers and they dyed hair and they pinched dough for piecrust, and they occasionally pressed against a little girl's forehead, checking for fever.

When I was very little, she wore a diamond ring, her engagement ring, on her left hand. It slipped off, many years ago, when she was washing dishes. Her ring went spiraling down the drain before she could fish it out of the soapy water, and she cried out for my dad to help. He took apart all the plumbing, but they never retrieved her ring. My mother cried and cried.

Over the course of a lifetime, she has wrung her hands in sorrow and she has clapped them together in great joy. And on the evening I was at my parents' house, watching my mom tie this bow, I remembered many more moments of clapping, many moments of joy.

She finished the bow and handed it over to me. "I hope this will work," she said.

I think it does. ◀

Outdoor Dreaming

IN THE SUMMERTIME, when I was a child growing up in Asheboro, I spent nearly every daytime hour in one of two outdoor places: either swaying from a hammock suspended between two heavy oaks in my grandmother's backyard, or pushing off from a white wooden swing that hung from the painted-blue ceiling of her front porch.

She lived in a tidy, white 1940s-era bungalow with a thick lattice of roses trailing up the east side and patches of clover mounding the front lawn. The blue porch ceiling, she explained to me, was to keep insects like wasps and yellow jackets from building nests up there.

"They see it as an extension of the sky," she said.

I learned a lot of outdoors folklore from her — that you can split the bark from a sweet gum and use it to brush your teeth or that a fig tree should be planted next to the side of a shed to shelter it from winter frost — but truth be told, I was more of a bookworm than any sort of a nature enthusiast.

One of the reasons I loved staying with my grandmother in the summer was that her house was across the street from the Randolph County Public Library and, at least twice a week, we walked over to stock up on books.

> I think she was grateful to have someone else out there, another body outside who kept the swing from sitting still.

I carted them to the porch, where I sat for hours in that swing, or to the hammock in the backyard, where I stretched out for so long, the tightly wound rope tamped deep indentations into the backs of my legs.

These were the days in which I discovered Judy Blume and S.E. Hinton and Lucy Maud Montgomery, devouring the stories of Margaret and Iggie and Deenie and Ponyboy. I read while my grandmother worked around the yard, weeding her garden or just resting on the concrete bench that anchored a row of her prized flowers, heavy-headed peonies, and gentle hydrangeas.

For her, there was no better place to be than outside, and after my grandfather died, I think she was especially grateful to have someone else out there to enjoy it with her, another body outside who kept the swing from sitting still, somebody else to help swat away flies and smell the sweetshrub growing wild.

What is it about being outdoors in North Carolina that creates such a powerful draw?

Maybe the answer is in that hammock, on those days my grandmother brought a book of her own out to the backyard, and the two of us laid side by side on that taut weave of rope, content to immerse ourselves in our own worlds and spend a small eternity drifting and staring up into the clouds — having been granted permission to do nothing and the freedom to do everything.

Those days are long gone, but often whenever I think of Anne of Green Gables or Ramona Quimby and all her exploits, I'm transported to the time of my childhood — and connected to my grandmother.

I still see her in the outdoor spaces, and when I think of her, I still look up toward the clouds, an extension of the sky.

Time Traveling in Seagrove

IN **1978, WHEN I WAS EIGHT YEARS OLD,** I took my first trip to Seagrove to visit the potteries. My aunt, Joanna, drove down to Asheboro from her home in Winston-Salem to pick up my grandmother and me. Joanna was an artist herself, and a collector, and she was taken with the potteries that were springing up in this small community in the southern part of our county.

I was excited for the trip. My parents ran a small business, which meant that there was no time for summer vacations. When other children were packing for the beach in mid-July, I was settling in to read my new round of comic books, so for me, the chance to go somewhere else — anywhere else — was thrilling.

Joanna had packed the car for an all-day outing: I shared the backseat with my younger cousin, Abe, and a picnic basket filled with deviled eggs, half a watermelon, and slices of homemade pound cake. We took the back roads to get to Seagrove, driving slow, and as soon as we crossed outside of Asheboro's city limits, we rolled down the windows, breathing deep the smell of sunshine and honeysuckle, open space and earth.

> ## Although we hadn't traveled more than 15 miles from home, it felt like we were very far away.

We drove down N.C. Highway 42 through Randolph County and ambled past the crumbling old farmsteads near Erect, their front yards taken over by thick-trunked magnolia trees, branches forgotten and hanging low, touching the ground. We passed wide swaths of pasture bordering the

roadside, overrun with pokeweed and field poppies, and I counted the scatterings of hay bales, coiled and fading tan in the mid-summer sun.

I watched as the terrain around us changed — fewer houses gave way to fields of horses and grazing cows, and, by the time we arrived at the first pottery studio — Jugtown — and turned into the long dirt driveway, dodging potholes and chickens, it was as though we had been transported through time. Although we hadn't traveled more than 15 miles from home, it felt like we were very far away.

In some ways, I suppose, we were.

Back then, there were only a dozen or so practicing potters — Jugtown, the Coles, and Auman's Seagrove Pottery Shop are the ones that stand out in my memory — and their studios were located right beside of their homes. Encouraged by the welcoming setting, we made ourselves at home, too, spreading out our lunch on a picnic table one of the potters had knocked together with old barn board,

and, afterward, Abe and I ran after the chickens, laughing and falling and brushing specks of gravel from our hands and knees.

I remember there were dogs — there were always lots of animals at the potteries — and we'd tentatively stick out our hands in front of the dog's noses, our offering of friendship.

On the days when the weather drove the chickens under the eaves, we'd go inside the shops and stand transfixed in front of the potters' wheels, watching as these craftsmen and women, hands stained the color of aged newspaper and forearms caked with dried clay, turned bowls and pulled handles for cups, the clay growing long beneath their fingers as if by magic. And it was magic, not only in how a craft was created, but also in how a community formed.

I visit this area often now — my pottery collection includes pieces from Luck's Wares, Nichols Pottery, Cagle Road, and Chris Luther. I've developed a love for this craft and its place in our region, and when I go back, it's as though I've gone far, far back, pulled deep into a place of memory, where the potters and farmers who make this community their home continue to bless us with their gifts from this rich earth. ◀

Old Family Photos

YOU'D THINK GROWING UP with a professional photographer at home — my dad owned Hudson Studios, a commercial photography studio in High Point from the late 1950s to the early '80s — that our house would have been filled with photographs.

Not so.

Aside from a few tabletop snapshots of my childhood dog, I don't remember a single framed photograph anywhere on the walls. At my friends' homes, school pictures and family portraits hung on the walls, and vacation pictures lined fireplace mantels. But in our house, there was no evidence that anyone had ever taken a photo of any kind.

I broke the unofficial "no photo" rule when, at about five or six years old, I wrote a letter to Santa Claus asking for my first camera. "All I want," I wrote, "is a camera where the picture comes out of the little hole." (Never mind that I actually spelled that last word "howl.")

That year, I got a Kodak Instant EK6, packaged in its bright yellow box, and several packs of instant film.

I carried that camera around everywhere, photographing anything in my path: stuffed animals on my bed; my parents while they were working, cooking, walking, turned away from me. Evidently, I wasn't particular about composition.

I kept this up for a while, and then I never gave those old instant photos much thought, until a few years ago, when I was home visiting.

My parents, paring down their lifestyle, had been going through old household inventory, weeding out the hodgepodge that accumulates after 30 years of living in the same place. In the process of reorganizing, they had moved a dozen or so cardboard boxes to a bookshelf downstairs.

My dad took that photograph before I was even born.

"What's in here?" I wondered, pulling one of the boxes off the shelf.

Inside were all my old photographs — 4-by-5 instant snapshots of Charlotte Hutchins, my best friend in the first grade; and pictures from my first trip to the mountains, taken from a car window, a faint ridge of treetops barely visible on the horizon. I still remember what it was like to peer across a scenic overlook for the first time, to glimpse the tiny cows and Monopoly-size houses contained in the world below, spread out before me in miniature. I was so captivated by the view, I could have looked at it forever.

There were other photos in that box, too. My dad as a young man with sideburns and a butterfly-collared shirt; my mom as a young woman 20 years younger than I am now, sitting by a pond with her back to the camera, her hair pulled into a ponytail and a fishing pole in her hand.

My dad took that photograph before I was even born.

And then there were the family photos: baby pictures I had never seen, my head barely lifting up from a white crib with yellow-flowered wallpaper in the background; photos of my grandmother and grandfather standing in a doorway at Christmastime, leaning in for a kiss beneath a plastic sprig of mistletoe; my parents and me at home during the ice storm of 1978, when we didn't have power for a week. We'd made pallets from quilts in front of the fireplace and, despite being cold and in the dark, the flashbulb from the camera illuminated our smiling faces, and we looked happy.

I spent hours sifting through these old photos, grateful for the opportunity to hear, in my mind, the voices and laughter from another time, reminding me why we take pictures in the first place — to keep our past present, and to preserve our world in views that stay with us forever.

Remembering Farmer School

N THE EIGHTH GRADE, I stood on stage in the auditorium of the old Farmer Elementary School, a bundle of nerves and kneesocks, and won the school spelling bee.

I don't remember the winning word, but I remember other details from that moment: how the plank floor of the auditorium shined with its fresh coat of varnish, applied the night before by the school custodian, Mr. Lee, a World War II veteran who wore overalls and never strayed far from his mop bucket; how the heavy green velvet curtain behind me on stage swayed whenever another student would walk to the microphone to spell; how the round metal clock in the entrance vestibule ticked away the minutes of what was surely an eternity. And I remember when it was over, how the entire student body erupted into applause.

I walked back to class buoyed by the cheers and good wishes from my teachers and classmates. It was the first time I felt that I hadn't let them down, like when I stood in the outfield during PE and chased softballs that rolled just out of my reach. On this day, for an hour anyway, I was a hero.

It was a moment I never forgot, and so when the elementary school finally retired from service about 18 years ago, I drove over to pay my respects to the old place.

Farmer School was built in 1924, a replacement for a schoolhouse that had burned earlier, and it had begun to deteriorate by the time I was a student there in the '70s. When I graduated high school, plans were underway to shutter the elementary school and build a new one a few miles away — one with whiteboards instead of chalkboards and security monitors instead of a check-in desk.

> I pulled on the door handle to the front entrance, and just like that, stepped back inside my childhood.

When I got to the school, I expected it to be boarded up, with No Trespassing signs taped to the doors.

But, aside from the conspicuous absence of school buses, the building didn't look abandoned; it just looked empty. As if it were merely waiting for the next round of students to clamber up the front steps, metal "Land of the Lost" lunchboxes knocking against their legs.

I pulled on the door handle to the front entrance, and just like that, stepped back inside my childhood.

Except for the echo of my footsteps, I wandered down the halls in silence, aware of the missing sounds — the pings of the steam radiators in the classroom, the punctuating taps of chalk on a blackboard — and then my mind began to fill in the empty space.

I heard the voice of Mrs. Hampton, my fourth-grade teacher, telling us to swish our mouths with the fluoride she'd pump into our paper cups; in the library, I heard the electronic beeps of the first computer I ever saw, an Apple II with its small green screen. I walked down to the basement cafeteria and remembered reaching down into the belly of the metal ice chest for a cardboard cup of ice cream, which I'd dig at with a tiny wooden paddle. On fall evenings, we children and our families would come back to this cafeteria for the school's classic chicken pie suppers, homecooked fundraising meals that were the highlights of community evenings.

Throughout its long history, Farmer School was populated with students whose parents were teachers, farmers, factory workers. We learned the basics here, sure, but we also learned from each other. We learned how to make friends, and we learned the names of our

neighbors. We learned to pull ourselves away from the concrete walls of the gymnasium and dance in the middle of the floor. We learned to take pride in our surroundings. We learned to celebrate our victories together.

This building has been unused for nearly 20 years now, and it's hard for me to think that, one day, it could disappear altogether. But the lessons this place held — well, that's what the school was intended for all along. Here, we learned what mattered, a lesson that will remain long after this old building is gone.

Hard Times, Good Times

ASK MY MOTHER ABOUT WORKING on the farm during tobacco harvest in the late 1950s, and she'll tell you about crawling out of bed before the sun came up so she could make it out to the barn before the first sled of tobacco came in.

She'll tell you about the ground lugs in the fields — those low-growing leaves of tobacco that have to be pulled first — and how clods of wet dirt cleaved to your skin and caked under your fingernails; how the leaves stained everything they touched with sticky, gummy, greenish tar.

By the end of the day, your hands would be coated with that tar, and to remove it, you'd have to squeeze a ripe tomato between your fingers, working the slick juices into your skin, letting the fruit's acid strip away the resin.

Ask her about working in the barn, and she'll tell you about how she started, at seven years old, first as a hander, gathering up three or four broad tobacco leaves at a time and handing them up to the stringer. She'll tell you about how she became a stringer herself, learning to loop, stringing tobacco methodically and fast. She developed her own way, her own rhythm that caused her to be one of the most sought-after stringers in rural southeastern Guilford County. Before she was even a teenager, my mother had daily jobs on neighboring farms, working for Richard Smith and the Clapps and the Barkers and the Shepards. She made 50 cents an hour until, one day, Mr. Smith proclaimed "Susie's too good to make just fifty cents," and so the farmers started paying her 75 cents.

It was a lot of money.

In autumn, at the end of barning season, she put all her money in a sack and rode in the car with her dad and two younger brothers to Elm Street in east Greensboro.

For everyone who worked here, the barn was entertainment.

While her dad waited, drinking beer inside the California Sandwich Shop, my mother and her two brothers walked across the railroad tracks to Meyers Department Store. Inside the entryway, steps led to the basement, where the discounted children's clothes were, and my mother used all her tobacco money to buy her school clothes for the year.

Ask her about the work in the barn, and she'll tell you that it wasn't all work; there were good times that carried them through the day. Before break time, her dad would go down the road in the truck to the store. He bought candy and moon pies and longneck bottles of RC Cola and Dr. Pepper. It was a special treat to have these snacks, and they'd all sit together beneath the shade trees beside the barn, taking long drags off those cold drinks.

For everyone who worked here, the barn was entertainment. My mother and her family had a television, a black-and-white set, and they watched "Perry Mason" and "Amos and Andy." But after that, in the country, a long way away from anything, what else was there to do? In the barn, the field hands gathered, the neighbors gathered, the family gathered, and this is where people visited with each other every day, working, yes, but also talking and laughing and singing old-time songs — "Keep on the Sunny Side" and "Will the Circle be Unbroken" — their voices working together, lifting toward the rafters, loud and strong and clear.

And at dinnertime — the noon meal — her grandmother, who had been cooking all morning, laid out a heavy spread of food — fried chicken and biscuits and milk gravy and big bowls of black-eyed peas and fried okra. The men ate first, and then everyone else, and afterward, they all went back to work, falling back into the cycle of production and harvest, one that has been repeated, on this farm and thousands of others across North Carolina, for generations, for centuries.

What We Ate

WHERE **I** GREW UP, we ate ripe figs right off the trees, and, in November, by the time the first frost had passed, we watched for the persimmons to fall. We'd hurry outside to gather them up from the ground, holding the fronts of our shirts out like aprons, toting the fruit inside the house where someone would grind the pieces, peel and all, into a pulp for persimmon pudding.

When the temperature dropped and the humidity went away, we could make fudge. The old recipe — the one my mother uses now, the one my grandmother used then — relies on the weather for its success: dense peanut butter fudge, airy divinity, and flats of chocolate spread into aluminum pans set up only when the weather is cooler, when there is a bite to the air.

bacon, fried in a cast-iron skillet, and eggs that had been scrambled in the drippings, flecked with brown bits.

On Saturday nights, we ate dinner at my grandparents' house. Chicken livers and salmon patties fried in my grandmother's old West Bend electric frying pan. After so many years of use, its Bakelite knob on the lid finally fell off, and my grandmother wove a plastic-bag bread tie through the hole so we'd have something to grab hold of.

My grandfather and I couldn't get enough of this food. We'd take turns lifting the lid on the electric skillet, burning our fingers and popping pieces of fried okra into our mouths, eating handfuls like candy.

There were days when my grandmother didn't feel well enough for cooking, and we went out instead,

We ate simple foods, modestly prepared.

We all had sweet tooths. We ate pound cake and licked the beaters — we didn't know to worry about raw eggs — and we ate pecan chess pie and banana pudding.

We ate homemade biscuits leavened with White Lily flour, split in two and covered with blackberry jelly. For breakfast, we ate strips of country

driving to Dixie III for a vegetable plate and cornbread or the Blue Mist for a barbecue sandwich or to the Apple House cafeteria in the Randolph Mall for chicken pie and carrot-and-raisin salad.

My grandfather always left the restaurants working the toothpick in his mouth, patting his stomach and saying how good the meal had been, no matter what we ate. When he died, and my grandmother followed, years later, we ate casseroles and potato salad. It got us through.

We ate simple foods, modestly prepared. Pimento-cheese sandwiches from my dad's own recipe, perfected from his days of running a sandwich shop. Boiled green beans and mashed potatoes with peppery brown gravy. Apples sliced in half and baked upside down until the flesh turns moist and the skins get slick with sugary juice.

On the day my dad went into the hospital for emergency open-heart surgery — valve replacement for a heart weakened by rheumatic fever as a boy — we didn't eat at all.

My mother and I sat in the hospital waiting room, scared and silent, until I finally went to the coffee shop and bought us two doughnuts. We weren't even hungry, but it occupied our hands and our minds until the doctor came out and told us, as we pushed back the taste of salty tears, how everything was going to be fine.

We went home that night, relieved and drained, and sopped leftover cornbread into glasses of milk before bed, turning the mixture into a paste that we ate with our spoons.

I don't remember anything ever tasting so good.

A Return to Christmas

N **1966, REPRISE RECORDS** released *The Dean Martin Christmas Album,* and by the time I discovered it at my grandparents' house, about 10 years later, I played it ceaselessly. I loved Dean's smooth rendition of "I'll Be Home for Christmas," and the winking lilt in his voice on "Marshmallow World." Hearing that music could make me believe it was snowing outside. It made me imagine I was grown up, and I would stand in the living room, pretending to be at a cocktail party, slinging one of my grandmother's silk scarves around my neck and clinking wine glasses filled with cranberry juice. It made me hope for a drop in the temperature so that the furnace in the basement would click on and push its heat up through the grate in the middle of the hallway, filling the house with warmth.

My grandparents had dozens of Christmas albums stacked beneath their Magnavox stereo, and every year, I'd select our soundtrack, kneeling in front of the record player in the living room, transfixed, as the voices from these records swirled around me.

I played Holiday Sing-Along with Mitch Miller and Nat King Cole's "The Christmas Song." There was Perry Como and the Fontane Sisters and Al Hirt and his blazing trumpet. I listened, again and again, to the Mormon Tabernacle Choir's innocent rendition of "Silent Night." In the background, everything we did — unwrapping ornaments from yellowed newspaper, dipping crocheted snowflakes in sugar water to stiffen them, taping holiday cards around the doorway in the kitchen — was set to music.

Watching a record spin on a turntable is mesmerizing. It's the twirl of figure skaters, smooth gliding movements across an ice-black lake. It's the pirouette of a ballerina atop a jewel box. It's the perpetual revolution of a Ferris wheel going around and around, lights sparkling against a deepening dark night.

> # I wanted to hear those sounds again, in the same way that I had listened as a child.

In later years, I stopped listening to music out loud. I got my first Walkman, and I kept the foam headphones strapped to my head at all times. I told myself the sound was better, that it was a more intimate musical experience to keep it all to myself. I forgot what the sound of a record was like — all crackle and texture, the hot hiss of the black space, atmospheric static, before the needle glides across the slim grooves and the music starts to play.

When my grandmother died 16 years ago, we sold all her records in a yard sale, boxing up the *Great American Songbook Collection* and Andy Williams and The Ray Conniff Singers for someone else to cart home and stash beneath a stereo. But we also sold her Billie Holiday and Ella Fitzgerald and one of my favorites, Bing Crosby's White Christmas. By that time, though, nobody had record players anymore, and we didn't think it mattered.

A few years ago, I started to miss that music.

I wanted to hear those sounds again, in the same way that I had listened as a child — out loud and filling the air. I bought a record player, and set it up in my living room. This year, I'll continue my search to accumulate those old records again. They're hard to find now; so many record shops have gone the way of furnace grates and silk scarves.

I keep my eyes open, though. I watch for yard sales, for boxes of records priced to sell from people who think it doesn't matter. I dig through bins at used shops, checking the vinyl for scratches and ruts.

I hope, one day, I'll find the ones I remember.

Wish You Were Here

SHORTLY AFTER **H**AWAII became the 50th state admitted to the Union, my great-aunt Hazel and her husband, Raymond, set off for their vacation of a lifetime.

They boarded a gleaming DC-8 bound for Honolulu, and for the first time in Hazel's life, she lifted her feet from North Carolina's soil.

After their two-week trip, Hazel and Raymond returned to their home in Asheboro with a suitcase full of mementos — a snow globe filled with two dancing Hula girls; folding paper fans printed with exotic orchids; postcards of swaying palm trees and candy-colored sunrises over the tropical beaches. For my great-Aunt, the trip ignited a newfound love for going places, and Hazel and Raymond took many more vacations after that.

Years later, before I was born, Raymond died, and Hazel lived the rest of her life in a second-floor apartment just off Asheboro's South Fayetteville Street.

I visited her often with my grandmother, and occasionally, I'd spend the night, packing my canvas Snoopy suitcase with pajamas and comic books.

Hazel was the first person I ever knew who lived in an apartment. She had a balcony that overlooked a small side street and a parakeet who lived in a fancy cage, two things that constituted big-city sophistication for me. A trip to Hazel's was a treat, a vacation from the everydayness of my rural Randolph County life.

I didn't grow up in a family that traveled very often; in fact, in their 40 years of marriage so far, my parents have taken exactly one vacation, in 1977, when the three of us went to the beach for a week. I don't remember much about that trip, other than the horseshoe shape of the motel rooms surrounding the swimming pool, and the fact that Elvis died midway through our stay. The AM radio in the motel room played Elvis songs for the rest of our trip.

> I could tell that there were times when she had gone somewhere in her mind.

My parents worked long hours, long days, and there was never any time or much money for travel. But somehow I still managed to go places and experience new things, even if it meant I found those experiences on the

second floor of a walk-up apartment.
Hazel didn't keep any child-friendly toys in her apartment, but we played cards, and we cooked together, and I read from her extensive collection of World Book encyclopedias about places I never expected to visit.

And although I never knew Hazel to travel anywhere after Raymond died, I could tell that there were times when she had gone somewhere in her mind, times when she cast her gaze outward and seemed to look very far away.

In the years before she died, I remember she liked to sit out on the balcony in the late afternoon, when it got the most sunlight, and feel the warmth on her face, on her skin that had become as thin as those Hawaiian paper fans. I'd sit with her out there, watching her tilt her head back as she closed her eyes and lifted her face toward the sun. I know she was thinking of Raymond then, and of their life together. I know she remembered their travels, when the two of them were young and happy. I can imagine her thoughts, the internal conversation we have with people who are no longer around. "The weather is beautiful, Raymond," I imagine her saying. "Wish you were here."

Game of Life

MY GRANDFATHER, Charles Harris Hudson, was a golfer. He wore a baby-blue bucket hat with tees stuck in the brim and walked around the house with a golf ball in his pocket, turning it over in his hands like a worry stone. Like many golfers who don't have the luxury of their own caddy, he often came home with lots of things tucked in his pockets: his leather golf glove, extra tees, folded score sheets, stubby pencils. In the winter, he'd stand over the heating grate in the hallway of the house and practice his putting stroke, padding his feet back and forth, back and forth, working his stance just right. By the first of March, he'd head for the golf course early in the morning, before the leagues arrived, stepping out onto fresh greens as untrammeled as new-fallen snow.

By the time I came along, my grandfather had been a lot of things in his life, but none of them had anything to do with golf.

He started out as a baseball player. In the 1930s, he played third base for an industrial league team, and he got an invitation — the dream of his life — to try out for the St. Louis Cardinals. He went to Missouri but got spiked in the knee during the first round of tryouts. It ended any hope he had of playing professional ball, and he came home, disappointed but true to his character, not dejected.

He switched his interest to tennis. He earned the nickname "Ace" by winning a Greensboro championship match. Meanwhile, during the war years, he was drafted into the Civil Service and became a welder. The government sent him to a shipyard

By the time I came along, my grandfather had been a lot of things in his life, but none of them had anything to do with golf.

He loved the game and, evidently, was good at it; I know he shot his age numerous times and won a couple of city tournaments — but I never knew what drew him to it.

in Virginia, where he helped build an aircraft carrier, the USS *Midway*, while my grandmother stayed home in North

Carolina with their three children. He didn't play anything during that time.

When he finished his service, he returned home, where his family now was living in Coleridge, and he began to make his living as a salesman. He sold BlueCross/BlueShield insurance, and he loved the work so much, he continued making sales calls well into his retirement. I remember when he'd put on a suit and lay his briefcase, stuffed with BlueCross pamphlets, across the front seat of his Oldsmobile. On those days, he'd leave the house to call on a customer, full of the anticipation of a sell, a win.

In 1982, my grandfather found out he had colon cancer. The doctors put him in the hospital; he had surgery, an awful kind, and then they sent him home. They gave him six months to live.

One morning, remarkably, he awoke with a sudden burst of energy. He got out of bed, dressed, and scrawled a note, in pencil, across the top of one his insurance envelopes.

"Don't worry about me," it read. "I'll be all right."

My grandfather stuck this note in between the salt-and-pepper shakers on the kitchen table and, without telling a soul, snuck out of the house and went to the golf course.

I have since learned that this spontaneous burst of energy with a terminal illness is common. And also short-lived. But on that day, he felt good. He put a few golf balls in his pocket, climbed behind the wheel of his Olds and drove to the golf course, his own place of peace, where he played and played until it was time, finally, to come home.

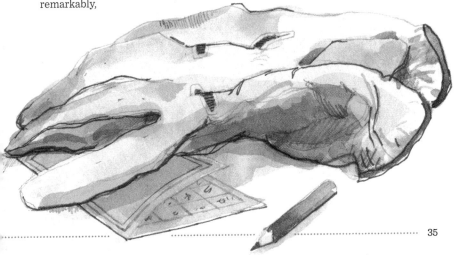

In Memory of Woods and Water

WHEN **I** WAS NINE YEARS **OLD,** my parents bought the first and only house they've ever owned, and we moved from our small rental in downtown Asheboro to the southwestern part of the county.

Out here, our house backed up to acres of dense woods, and a long dirt road sliced the edge of our backyard, snaking up a long hill toward the few other houses that were sequestered in the rural landscape.

On the day we moved, I walked the length of that dirt road, about a mile from top to bottom, in hopes that someone my age lived nearby. It was a solitary walk, and before I gave up and went home, I gouged out a message in the dirt road with a stick. "Hi," I scraped in the dirt. "I am looking for a friend." I scrawled my name, "Elizabeth," and drew an arrow to my house.

It retrospect, it was a silly thing to do. Of course, I didn't foresee the fleeting nature of writing in dirt — one slight gust of wind or a pickup truck barreling down the road would have wiped clean my hopeful call for friendship, but evidently, that didn't happen.

For some reason, my message stayed, and the next day, Krista Payne, a neighbor who had been riding her bicycle down the road, knocked on our back door.

Krista was about my age, one grade below me, and she lived with her younger brother and parents in the house nearest ours, on the other side of the dirt road. She had seen my message, and had come to the house to meet me.

Krista and I became instant friends, and we spent long hours together, swinging on her porch and throwing a ball with her brother and retreating to our deep woods, where our imaginations took root. Here, we

> We tossed pebbles into the water and stared at the lazy ripples in the slow-moving current.

pretended that the towering pine trees were the walls of our house; the rotting stumps were our chairs. We rode on fallen-log horses and fought mystical branch creatures. On foot, we chased each other through tangled weeds, edging deeper in, eventually stumbling down the slope of a hill to come upon an ankle-deep, clear-water creek.

Krista and I were drawn to the water. We spent early Saturday mornings at the creek, plunging our hands in up to our wrists, pretending to pan for imaginary gold like we had learned to do at Reed's Gold Mine. After a rain, we'd watch for tiny toads, and on the hottest days, we pushed up our pants legs to wade in the water, holding on to each other's shoulders, our breath catching with those first cold steps. We laughed a lot.

Then we got older. Instead of wading in the water, we'd sit on granite boulders that had somehow worked their way out of the earth. Our conversations changed from make-believe houses to less childish topics — boys and school and hopes and fears. We tossed pebbles into the water and stared at the lazy ripples in the slow-moving current. We watched as the detritus of nature drifted toward some other place, toward a larger stream, maybe, eventually moving toward some ancient, nameless river. We never knew where the water came from, and now, I wish we'd looked. I wish we'd walked along the water's edge, searching for where it came from and following it where it led.

Eventually, of course, Krista and I drifted. We grew up; we moved away. The dirt road that ran between our houses has long since been paved and the woods have been mostly cleared, infiltrated with other development. As I write this, the foundation for another house sits in the middle of it all. It's hard for me to look at.

I cope with the changes by hoping that whoever moves here, when this new house is finally completed, has a child who is eager to explore the rooms of these woods, someone who will catch a glimpse of the creek's shimmer through the brush, and chase it to its source, running alongside as its current — and all the things it carries — rushes by.

A Season of Promise

ON THE STREET WHERE **I** LIVE, a massive white oak anchors the edge of my neighbor's yard. The tree is at least 100 years old, or it was anyway, until it finally fell recently, the victim of weakness or disease or maybe just old age.

On the day it fell, we all heard it hit.

It struck the earth like cannon fire, carrying with it a lifetime of history — battle scars from ferocious summertime thunderstorms and winter icing, remnants of birds' nests built in its upper limbs, specters of long-ago children playing beneath it, tagging it as home base in front-yard ballgames and swinging from its branches.

On the day it fell, we — the whole neighborhood — came rushing out of our homes to see what had happened and to stare at this giant, whose upturned roots spilled out from its underside like entrails.

We stood around its wide canopy that had shielded our street from the hottest days of summer, disbelieving that this icon, this symbol of our neighborhood, was no more.

> We were struck with the realization that, in nature, nothing stays the same.

On the day it fell, we felt this loss. The tree lay lifeless across the neighbor's yard and into the street, and nobody knew what to do. We edged close to it, tentatively, as if this behemoth might somehow, suddenly, lift its limp branches to rise up and right itself.

On the day it fell, we were struck with the realization that, in nature, nothing stays the same.

This tree was one of the reasons I love living where I live: It reminded me of what this area of Guilford County must have looked like a century ago, before development cut deep, before my 1970s-era cul-de-sac was carved out of what was once, before anyone arrived, a dense oak forest.

I'm reminded of this former landscape when I take my morning walk through the neighborhood in the springtime. Our acidic soil, enhanced by so many acorns, deepens the blue in the clusters of hydrangeas that I see from house to house and encourages a delirious production of azaleas. I've often believed the azaleas in Greensboro are the most vibrant anywhere, and I think it's because of that oaky soil.

White oaks like the one that fell in my neighborhood have a significant place in Greensboro's history. One of the Cone Mills' textile plants was named the "White Oak Plant" because of the 200-year-old tree that stood on the property. That manufacturing plant became one of the largest indigo dyeing operations in the world; it needed 10 warehouses just for its inventory and even had its own power plant. Even now, there is so much that has survived with the "white oak" name: entire neighborhoods, city streets, plenty of churches, even a lake.

Today, I walked the neighborhood for the first time after a long, cold winter. It was 60 degrees and sunny, a mid-winter tease of spring. I walked past the house no longer in the shadow of the white oak. It's strange to see this altered landscape, but I'm getting used to it. For years, the view from the street was a towering tree. But now, instead of seeing the thick swath of green leaves overhead, I see brilliant blue sky, opening up to a realm of possibilities. It's just as beautiful.

The Saltwater Cure

WHEN **I** WAS NINE YEARS OLD, jumping around in the old woodshed behind my grandmother's house, I took a splinter, two inches long, right in the toe.

I ran inside in tears, hopping and holding my foot so she could see the jagged shard deep beneath the skin.

It wasn't my first splinter. Or my last. But this was different. It needed something more than tweezers.

My grandmother ran warm water in a wash bucket and poured in about a quarter of a box of salt from the Morton's container.

She told me to sit there, on the edge of the kitchen chair, with my foot immersed in the bucket for about a half an hour. I was fidgety, focused on the pain in my toe. "Be still," she said, "and let the water do its work."

Before long, the water had not only numbed my sore toe, but also the splinter had worked its way out. The next time I looked down into the salty water, it was drifting to the bottom of the bucket.

It was my first lesson in learning about salt water's capacity to mend.

I've used this trick ever since to remove splinters, soothe a sore throat,

I thought about what it means to be connected to the water, to the ocean.

wash out a cut. I have no idea whether this treatment is medically sound, but it seems to make things better, and that's good enough for me.

A few years ago, I was reminded of the restorative power of salt water during a trip to the beach.

After what had been a long and weary drive from Greensboro, I landed at the Yacht Basin Provision Company, a seafood shack in Southport.

Here, the salty sea air had taken its toll, seasoning the wooden structure and adding a patina of rust to the propane tanks that sit outside the door. Inside, I ordered a yellowfin tuna sandwich off the chalkboard menu and walked out to the open-air deck overlooking the waterway to eat it.

Strains of Willie Nelson singing "Sitting on Top of the World" played over the sound system. Pelicans dipped in and out of the water from the dock, and boats skimmed nearby, a reminder of the omnipresent fishermen, who, on their daily journey of ocean and sky, make their life from this salty sea.

I sat here for a couple of hours and thought about what it means to be connected to the water, to the ocean. I thought about its immense history. About its power to restore, to heal, to mend. About how, as Carl Sandburg said, "it must know more than any of us." More than anything, I think, it knows how to calm and soothe our souls.

When we are still and let it do its work.

Freedom on Two Wheels

> I remember what it felt like. It was independence, newfound freedom — and fright.

MY FIRST BIKE was a cobalt blue Schwinn Fair Lady, the girl's version of the classic StingRay. It had plastic streamers that flapped from its high-rise handlebars and a wide, white banana seat, and I loved it.

I rode it as fast as the training wheels would let me, mostly around the gravel parking lot that was behind my mom's needlework shop on Fayetteville Street in Asheboro.

One day in June, my dad told me we were going to take off the training wheels. It was time, he said, for me to learn how to ride on my own. I watched as he laid the bike down on its side and worked the wheels off with a wrench. He righted the bike, patted the seat, and told me to hop on.

I was unsure of this. Scared that I wouldn't be able to balance. Scared I would fall.

Dad held onto the bike while I swung my leg over and put my feet on top of the studded pedals.

I wobbled. My dad gripped the back of the bike, keeping it upright so I wouldn't topple over. Then he started running behind me, holding me steady and pushing me forward at the same

time. He was saying, "Now, pedal — pedal!" And I did. I pumped my legs and the front wheel started to weave erratically.

Then, somehow, the bike straightened up. Now, I was pushing the pedals with my feet, and I was moving, not wobbling.

The moment I felt like I had control of the bike, I turned around, expecting to see my dad right there, with his hand on the back.

But he was far away, standing in the middle of the gravel lot, watching me go.

I remember feeling a sense of surprise that I was on my own — I was actually riding a bike by myself — and then I saw him grinning, laughing, raising his hands over his head, and waving wildly at me. He was yelling, "Hold on! Hold on!"

And I did.

I remember what it felt like. It was independence, newfound freedom — and fright. The security and safety those extra wheels provided were gone; the security and safety my dad provided were, too.

But in that moment, when I looked over my shoulder, I also saw his excitement and pride.

I look back now, and I think, "How did he do it?" How did he bring himself to release his hold on me, his only child, there in that gravel driveway? Knowing that I could very well fall. Knowing that I could very well fail.

How do fathers manage to let go? How do they stand back when their children, their only sons, their only daughters, drive a car or go on a date for the first time? How do they watch their children pack up and go off to college for the first time, where they could very well fall, where they could very well fail?

How do they let go and move out of the way when the boxes get packed, when the children move away, get married, ride off into the distance?

And yet, somehow, they do.

One day in June, my dad let go of the back of the bike, and he taught me to ride all by myself. He held me steady and pushed me forward, at the same time.

Maybe it takes the same kind of courage to let go as it does to hold on.◀

The Best Sandwich

A **FEW MONTHS AGO,** I had lunch with my mom in the break room at her work.

It was her 60th birthday, and I'd offered to take her out, anywhere she wanted. She told me that she'd rather eat the sandwich she'd brought from home.

Initially, I wasn't sure why she didn't want to go out — we should do something special on her birthday, I thought. But so she wouldn't have to eat alone, I packed a lunch for myself and joined her.

As I unwrapped my peanut butter and jelly — simple, nothing fancy — my mom pulled her lunch from a paper sack. Ham and cheese. To anyone else, it was ordinary. But as soon as I saw it, I remembered something about my parents that I'd forgotten.

Every day, my dad packs my mom's lunch for her. He's been doing this for years, ever since he retired. There's a method to his sandwich construction, and I could see how carefully he went about it: five thin slices of meat — I know he would have counted the slices — layered with cheese and stacked between two pieces of soft bread, each one spread with a deliberate amount of mayonnaise. He had also included a handful of potato chips, folded neatly in Saran Wrap, two oatmeal cookies, and a little Tupperware tumbler of sweet tea.

We ate quietly, contentedly. I could see how happy she was, how much it meant to know that someone thought enough to put together a lunch bag for her. "It's good," my mom said, nodding between bites.

And I knew it was.

To anyone else, my mom's meal would have been forgettable, but as I watched her eat, and saw her enjoyment, I realized what went into the making of this lunch.

Thirty years ago, my dad opened a small sandwich shop, a place called Phil's, in downtown Asheboro.

He had the menu standards — foot-long hot dogs and hamburgers — but what made the place special was his homemade sandwich-food fare. Grilled pimento cheese. Chicken salad. Egg salad. These were his own recipes, each one spiked with a special ingredient to add flavor (like extra sweet-pickle juice drizzled into the tuna fish).

My dad worked hard to prepare such unassuming food. I remember the long nights he spent hunched over our dining room table at home, hand-chopping pounds of chicken into small pieces and grating blocks of cheddar cheese by hand.

> Back then, we all ate where the food was familiar, where we knew what we were going to get.

My dad's sandwich shop was a good place, a welcoming place, a place people could get a good lunch for a fair price. Simple. Nothing fancy.

Back then, we all ate where the food was familiar, where we knew what we were going to get. We ate at the Blue Mist and the Little Dipper and Hop's Barbecue. We ate at Little Castle on Sunset Avenue. Even now, I can taste those cheeseburgers at Little Castle.

Juicy meat, a flattop bun — the old-timey kind — glistening with grease from the grill.

When I was in high school, Amy McBride and I started every Friday night the same way. We settled into a booth inside Sir Pizza and ordered our favorite, a medium ham-and-pepperoni pizza and two diet Cokes. It's what we liked. It's what we knew.

There is comfort in the familiar. A sandwich sliced the right way. A warm pickle pressed on top of bread, softening a circle beneath it. The crumple of parchment paper around a cheeseburger. The recognizable whoosh of a bun steamer. We know what's coming next. And we look forward to it. Something simple. Nothing fancy.

Two months ago, I went home to visit my dad for his 73rd birthday. When I walked into the house, he was already pulling a container of egg salad from the refrigerator. He makes a great sandwich. I know many of his secrets, yet I can't figure out what he does to food that makes it taste so good. It's something I can't seem to replicate in my own home. Somehow, I suspect it doesn't have anything to do with the food itself. I think my mom knows that, too.

"Can I make you some lunch?" he asked me.

I couldn't think of any meal I'd enjoy more.

Brewing Sunshine in a Gallon Jar

MANY YEARS AGO, WHILE MY parents were working long hours running their shop, I spent my summer days at my grandmother's house. We read books and went for a walk every day, stopping at neighbors' houses for something to drink and to admire their flower gardens. We fried okra and clipped laundry to the clothesline and, in late afternoons, we sat in the porch swing, kicking our feet just enough to keep it swaying, to keep the breeze going.

By August, summer moved in slow motion, and when the sun finally shot the temperatures into the 90s, the heat whipped us. We stopped using the stove to cook. We stayed inside, confined to the one room in the house that had a box-unit air conditioner mounted in the window. We stuck our faces up to it and breathed in the shock of cold air. We froze bananas and ate them like popsicles to stay cool, and we soaked towels in ammonia spirits and draped them across our necks.

One afternoon, while flipping through the stack of Good Housekeeping magazines my grandmother kept in a basket on the floor, I came across a recipe for Lipton Sun Tea. I took the page to my grandmother and asked if we could make it.

She already had the tea bags, of course — in fact, we already had tea; my grandmother always had a fresh pitcher in the refrigerator — but neither of us could deny the appeal of something as simple as brewing our favorite beverage in the sun.

That day, she took me to Rose's, a discount store in town, and we bought a special Sun Tea jar, one with a yellow screw-top lid and a spigot to release the tea. Back at home, we filled it up with water, put in three family-size tea bags and set the jar on the concrete walkway, taking advantage of our newfound use for the sweltering August heat.

We checked on our concoction every 15 minutes, tilting the jar from side to side.

Then we just waited. We willed the clouds to stay away. We laughed about how our sun tea would turn into cloud tea, and nobody wanted that. We checked on our concoction every 15 minutes, tilting the jar from side to side. We drank glasses of our already-made tea from the refrigerator, and, while it was sweet and delicious, we were convinced that it would be inferior to what was sitting outside in the sun, if for no other reason than the sheer time it was taking.

Gradually, the sides of the jar heated up, and the water began to tint a deep amber color, like resin or syrup, taking on a rich bronze hue as if the sun itself had permeated the jar.

It took all day. By dinnertime, we finally proclaimed it "done" and poured ourselves a glass. The tea was warm and melted the ice in our glasses, and it went down sweeter and more delicious than anything I'd ever had. We drank nearly the entire jug in one sitting, going back to the spigot for more, saying how, yes, it was worth the wait, the way so many good things, done simply, are.

When I look back now, I can remember the ease of those long summer days, and how the simplest activities enacted beneath the blaze of an August sky — searching for four-leafs in a patch of clover; smelling approaching rain just before a storm; brewing sunshine in a gallon jar — were the most fulfilling.

It's no wonder we stretched them out for as long as possible. ◀

History Among Us

MY PARENTS HAVE COLLECTED ANTIQUES for as long as I can remember. Growing up, our house was filled with interesting objects: metal scales and vintage thermometers, pewter tavern plates with thick silversmith marks etched into the bottom, blue spongeware pitchers.

As a kid, though, I had no use for these old things.

Then, one day, I began to collect community cookbooks, the older the better.

I liked the recipes, of course, but more than that, I liked how you could read a town — how you could tell the story of a place — based on the recipes in the books. One of my favorites, *The Pennsylvania State Grange Cookbook,* circa 1940, uses ingredients my Southern kitchen has never seen: Huckleberry pudding? And a closer reading of *Favorite Recipes of the Carolinas: Meats,* published about 45 years ago, gives a glimpse of what people were cooking in, say, Sophia. I may not ever make Mrs. Marvin Staley's Quail Pie, but I love knowing that she did.

I can read cookbooks like these and see a kitchen just as it was many years ago, before chickens became boneless and skinless. My old cookbooks all have home remedy sections, too, because kitchens then were like apothecaries. And the books are practical. I've learned how to set a complicated table from the diagrams in these old books.

By now, I probably have

enough in my collection, and yet, I keep thinking I'll look for just one more.

I find some of the best ones at the Liberty Antiques Festival each year.

On the first weekend in autumn and again in the spring, 100 acres of farmland off U.S. Highway 421 transform into a setting for one of the largest antiques festivals in the state. It's truly something to see: About 400 dealers haul in their goods in long trailers and on the beds of pickup trucks.

> These are the relics of another lifetime, things that all once had a home someplace else.

I go to the festival every year with my mom. These days, my parents are collecting less — in fact, as they downsize their life, my mom is looking to get rid of many of her antiques — but we enjoy browsing the aisles and eating barbecue sandwiches and looking at all the things that once belonged to other people.

All things have their history, their provenance — and it's easy to get lost in their past. You can see it in those old cookbooks, or in a brown owl McCoy cookie jar, or in a milk-glass lamp, or in the metal lunch buckets that still smell like wrapped peanut butter and jelly sandwiches. These are the relics of another lifetime, things that all once had a home someplace else.

I can imagine their settings. I can imagine the story of their place.

An old typewriter tells of a smoky office, of carbon-copied letters pounded out on letterpress stationery, the fast zwippt the roller makes when the paper is removed; vintage Mason jars tell of hot days spent canning, of blanching tomatoes and peaches in boiling water before putting them up, of sealing jars of beans and okra and setting them on a back porch, readying for a hard winter ahead.

I can imagine the stories held within a tray of antique wedding rings, platinum bands with engravings still visible, full of so much promise and anticipation.

All things that were once part of a future.

Now part of the past.

I like to think that we can find a new place for these old things, these things that have endured throughout one lifetime already. I like to think we can create our own stories for them. And let them become part of our history, too.

Blessings of Peace

BORN AND RAISED in the heart of North Carolina's Quaker Belt, my grandmother, whose maiden name was Allen, could trace her religious roots way back, to the earliest Quaker settlers in the area and even beyond that, all the way to the Irish Quakers before they migrated to Pennsylvania.

When I was small, she'd tell me stories about growing up as a young girl in the early 1900s in her church in Ramseur, Holly Spring Friends Meetinghouse.

After she married and moved to Asheboro, she continued to attend Holly Spring, but in her later years, and after my grandfather died, driving too far on the back roads of Randolph County to get there just wasn't an option. She found her place of worship closer to home, at Asheboro Friends Meeting.

When I was about 9 years old, I started going to church with her. I looked forward to every Sunday, to putting on a dress and carrying my white Bible — the one engraved with my initials — my first gift from her when I was born. My parents, who had to open their shop on Sunday morning in Randolph Mall, would drop me off at her house, and she'd drive us the short four blocks to the church. When we parked, I'd come around to the driver's side of the car and help her out. Although she was still capable of driving, she had become unsteady on her feet, and it reassured her to be able to hold onto me.

Quaker churches, if you've never been to one, are small on ceremony. There aren't any stained-glass windows or any elaborate ornamentation. The music is modest. To my grandmother, this was important. She lived her life plainly, finding peace in the simplest of places: among the rose bushes in her backyard or in her small kitchen, quietly assembling ingredients for one of her golden pound cakes.

Asheboro Friends Meeting had a pastor, and we listened to the short sermon each Sunday. Afterward, I remember there was time set aside for anyone in the church to stand and speak. "If the spirit calls you," the old-timers would say.

My grandmother would drop her head and say silent prayers.

Often, nobody would speak, and we'd just sit quietly for what was called silent worship.

My grandmother would drop her head and say silent prayers. She'd talk, I think, to my grandfather, and she'd pray for the health of her family, for my mom and dad, for me. Sometimes, during this silent worship, she'd slip me a piece of candy, usually an unwrapped buttermint. There was no noisy wrapper to deal with, and as she'd transfer the candy into my hand, I'd carefully pop it in my mouth without anyone seeing, happy and convinced that the two of us shared a secret no one else knew about.

Although my grandmother loved the services at Asheboro Friends, her heart never left Holly Spring, and that's where she was buried, 15 years ago, alongside my grandfather, who died 10 years before she did.

I hadn't been to Holly Spring since her funeral, A few days ago, I drove down there. I pulled into the small, gravel driveway leading to the cemetery, and I got out of the car and walked around.

It was unbelievably quiet.

I saw the Hudson tombstone with her name — Norva Allen — and my grandfather's — Charles "Ace" — carved side by side. I saw the other markers for the Allen family — my family — small and worn, with dates from the 1800s still barely visible. And there were other stones, too, names I've known all my life: Hinshaw and Stout, Craven and Cox.

I've always thought church cemeteries were beautiful places — there's a reverence among these grounds that doesn't exist anywhere else — and at Holly Spring, maybe because it carries such a deep history, maybe because I felt so connected to my roots, I was overcome with emotion.

I wish I'd had a piece of candy just then, something to pop in my mouth, something to ease the lump in my throat.

I got back in the car and drove home, grateful for the family and friends that have shaped my life, and most of all, thankful in my heart for these profound places of peace.

Window Shopping

YEARS BEFORE THERE WAS A **MALL** on the highway and before the big-box stores cropped up on Dixie Drive, everyone in Asheboro went downtown to do their Christmas shopping. My grandmother lived a few blocks from downtown, and a few days before Christmas, we'd walk to Sunset Avenue to see all the window displays.

The window at Belk-Yates was my favorite. Every year, the store created a magical Christmas scene: mechanical elves hammered out toys in a never-ending rhythm, Styrofoam snowflakes dangled from fishing line, and soft-eyed reindeer tilted their heads up and down. But the best part was all the lights. Dozens of strands of Christmas lights — each one its own tiny, twinkling star — wound around the window, framing the whole display in brightness and warmth. Those lights spilled out beyond the window, illuminating the entire sidewalk, and I could see, in the window's reflection, how my grandmother and I glowed.

I loved it all so much. Everything about this scene was exactly how I'd imagined the North Pole, and I stood transfixed in front of this window for as long as my grandmother would let me, tingling with excitement.

After Belk-Yates, we'd head to Eagle's Five and Dime, where we'd take a break from the chilly air and go inside.

Eagle's was a store unlike any I'd ever been in. It didn't sell just one thing, like clothing or jewelry. It had everything anyone could ever want. It had clothing and small kitchen appliances, such as blenders and fondue pots. It had gardening items and beauty supplies, such as Jean Nate body spray and Coty face powder.

> ## Stuffed animals and board games crowded the shelves that stretched nearly to the ceiling.

It also had the best toy department in town. Stuffed animals and board games crowded the shelves that stretched nearly to the ceiling. Sleds and wagons hung overhead, suspended by chains from the metal beams, leaving valuable floor space for other things, like Big Wheels and toy kitchens.

I'd wander the aisles of the toy department searching the shelves for things I wanted, things I hoped would find their way under the Christmas tree at home: the Operation game, an Etch-A-Sketch, a Mrs. Beasley Doll, a

Wooly Willy magnetic game.

On our way out of the store, we'd pass by my other favorite section: the long, glass candy counter, behind which were dozens of bins of bulk candy. There were Bit-O-Honeys and Necco wafers and orange jelly slices. There were malted milk balls and Lemon Drops coated with sugar. My grandmother would hand me a dollar bill, and I'd get a small paper bag of my favorite candy on earth: Brach's chocolate stars. These were dollops of creamy milk chocolate, in a star shape, and they were, without a doubt, the best candy that had ever been created.

After Eagle's, we'd keep walking, past Eva Fry's clothing store, where we'd admire the lean, graceful mannequins in heavy fur coats; past Grime's jewelers, where we'd peer in at the watches on display, at the sparkling diamond rings that sat in their tiny boxes. My grandmother would make up stories about the ladies who might get those diamond rings on Christmas Eve. She'd tell me how the men might propose and where they'd spend their honeymoons.

We giggled at our stories and walked arm in arm down the street, my grandmother and I, marching in our own little Christmas parade. We'd walk back home, eating our candy right out of the bag and letting the twinkling lights fade behind us.

Eagle's is, of course, long gone now, and Belk-Yates relocated to the Randolph Mall out on the highway nearly 30 years ago. It's an open storefront, and there's no window for mechanical displays. These days, there are so many more shopping choices, so many places to go. But whenever I drive down Sunset Avenue, I see the same buildings that used to house these stores, and I remember what it was like to stand in front of all those windows, in the glow of a childhood made so happy with lights and toys and a small bag of candy shaped like stars.

The Morning Meal

IT WAS EARLY IN THE MORNING, still dark outside, and I came down the stairs at The Castle Bed and Breakfast at Silver Lake in Ocracoke a few hours before breakfast, a few hours, still, before most of the guests had gotten up.

I thought I might find a cup and some hot water for tea in the inn's kitchen. I figured it was too early to hope for coffee, but when I walked into the room, I was surprised to find another woman, Gladys Stover, already there, standing behind the counter, in front of the sink. She was adjusting an apron over her clothes.

"Good morning," she said as I walked in, with the warmest lilt you've ever heard in someone's voice, greeting me with a genuine smile and the first words I heard that day.

Gladys was working — she's one of the regular breakfast cooks at The Castle — and it was easy to see how quickly she became immersed in the rhythm of the morning. She'd already made a pot of coffee for early risers like me and assembled the ingredients for biscuits. She was about to start mixing batter for French toast. And as I stood there for a few minutes, warming my hands on a coffee mug, watching her pull crates of eggs out of the refrigerator and turn on burners on the stove, I realized I'd found the inspiration for our first breakfast issue, something we had not done before in *Our State* magazine.

I loved watching Gladys work in her kitchen, and I wanted readers to see what I saw: a hard worker. An early riser. Someone who takes a great deal of pride in what she puts out there for other people to enjoy.

It's the person behind the breakfast that makes it matter.

For people in North Carolina, breakfast has always been a special meal. Our strong agricultural roots meant farmers who got up before sunrise, workers who depended on a hearty meal to carry them through the morning. Fresh eggs. Thick bacon. Pancakes and grits and country potatoes and homemade strawberry preserves canned in the summer and opened at the table in the winter, the jar bursting with the memory of a brighter season and a reminder that, in the midst of a cold winter, bountiful days will return.

We feel a connection to our breakfast foods, certainly — sausage from our pigs, eggs from our chickens, ingredients grown right beneath our feet, on our own land — but more important, we feel a kinship to those people who take time to prepare our meals. Seeing Gladys in the kitchen in Ocracoke, spending her morning cooking for grateful guests, reminded me why breakfast holds such significance to us, why we think of it as the most personal meal of the day. It's the person behind the breakfast that makes it matter.

For me, the best breakfast was the eggs that my grandmother scrambled in bacon drippings, cooked on those mornings after I'd spent the night with her, keeping her from loneliness the year my grandfather died.

It was the waffles and sausage at the Golden Waffle after sunset, a much-anticipated breakfast-for-dinner treat whenever my Uncle Garland, long gone now, visited from Ramseur.

It was the country-ham biscuit from the drive-through of The Biscuit Co. on the winter mornings when snow canceled school, but my parents had to keep their shop open anyway. I was too young to stay home by myself, so the three of us — my mom, my dad, and I — piled into my dad's pickup truck and braved the slick roads, stopping on the way at The Biscuit Co. for something good. Something filling. Something comforting. Something warm.

These are the breakfasts that carry us through our days, the breakfasts that carry us, really, through our lives.

These are what give us our good mornings.◄

Who We Are

THE RANDOLPH ROOM at the Asheboro Public Library is crammed with all the materials anyone would need for historical or genealogical research. File cabinets and bookcases are filled with marriage records and old land deeds, newspapers and church records, library scrapbooks, Ellis Island Immigration books, and Sanborn Fire Insurance maps. There are high school yearbooks from the county's schools. There are thick, leather-bound books stuffed with cemetery and census records.

And then there's the shelf full of old City Directories.

Until I saw them sitting there, on my recent visit to the library, I'd forgotten all about these books and how much time I spent reading them when I was a kid. My grandfather, who was a life insurance salesman, ordered an updated directory every year, and when it came, I'd sneak away with it and spend hours poring over the pages, reading each entry the way some kids read dictionaries or World Atlases.

The City Directory was just like a phone book, but better. Aside from names, addresses, and phone numbers, it listed what someone did for a living and where he worked, his wife's name and job, if she was employed, how many people lived in the home, whether someone was retired. They were like condensed personal histories of everyone in town, and I guess it helped my grandfather in his business to know a little something about the people he called on.

The directory told the story of the people who lived in the town: the supervisor at Klopman Mills who owned a home on Redding Road, the sawmill worker in Central Falls, the brick mason in Franklinville, the pastor at Seagrove United Methodist Church.

> I loved knowing about people, even people I'd never know. I still do.

Job descriptions were abbreviated, and I liked figuring out what "mgr" or "loom clnr" meant.

There were listings for a "wtrs" at Sea King Fish Camp, for a detective at Randolph County Sheriff's Department, for an "assemblr" at G.E., and for a "maint man" at Union Carbide.

A weigher at Yates Country Ham.

A stockroom employee at Stedman Furniture.

A switchboard operator at First National Bank.

I can't imagine why, at 7 years

old, any of this was interesting to me, but I loved it.

I loved knowing about people, even people I'd never know. I still do.

When I read through these directories now — Asheboro's collection goes back to 1937 — I see more than a listing of names. I see a portrait of a place.

So many local business names emerge — Acme-McCrary, Glenn Raven Mills, B.B. Walker Shoe Company — that it's easy to pinpoint Asheboro's identity: a hard-working town, blue-collar built. A family place. A compact community.

I can almost see, too, what these listings didn't say: that the maintenance man at Union Carbide was also a World War II United States Army veteran; that the waitress at Sea King Fish Camp just finished her associate's degree at what was then Randolph Tech; that the farmer, whose address was listed simply as "Route 4," lost his wife.

Of course, I don't know these details for sure. But because of the descriptions, I could think of these people as more than names in a phone book. They held jobs and had families and owned homes. When you know what people do, you can understand the story of who they are.

And they stop being faceless names on a page or anonymous entries in a book.

They become real.

They become people we know.

A House Filled

MY PARENTS TALK OF MOVING out of their house, the house I grew up in, the house they built 32 years ago.

It's just the two of them now, and they're getting weary of the amount of work it takes to keep a house up — to wash the windows, to carry laundry up and down stairs, to dislodge the wasp nests that form under the eaves, to keep the yard mowed and raked.

And so, maybe, they say, it's time to find a home that's more manageable, more efficient, a place better suited to their needs.

I know it's not an easy decision to come to, to leave a place filled with so many memories, so much history.

I remember when this house was being built, before it had any history at all. My parents and I would drive out every week to check on it, excited to see what sort of progress had been made on our new home.

It was out in the country, at the foot of the Uwharrie Mountains, where the land just starts to lift. We'd drive past Yates Country Ham and make the turnoff toward Farmer,

past sprawling fields filled with cows and horses. When we got to the unfinished structure that would, in a few months, become our home, we'd climb out of the car and excitedly slip in between the framework of the rooms, breathing in sawdust and imagining how it was all going to come together.

I remember my parents beaming with optimism for the future.

Without its walls in place, the house looked bigger than the small rental we were living in. I remember my parents beaming with optimism for the future, looking at their blank slate and wondering aloud how we'd ever fill it all up.

Over the years, of course, we did.

Go inside the house now, and you'll see evidence of a full life. Old scales and thermometers hang in the den, reminders of my parents' once-thriving fervor for antiques. A large needlework sampler, once displayed in my mom's craft store, decorates the hallway. My grandmother's china cabinet stands in the corner of the dining room, holding a collection of Seagrove pottery; a wall of cabinets in a spare bedroom holds my dad's cameras and equipment from the photography studio he had many years ago.

This house is filled with so much.

It's filled with the smell of Saturday afternoon fried chicken and milk gravy and Wednesday meat loaf and my dad's spaghetti sauce simmering on the stove. It's filled with the oily aroma of lighter fluid and charcoal burning on the grill in the summertime.

It's filled with the lazy light of afternoon streaming through the windows. Our dog, Muffin, loved to lie on the floor and warm her back in a pool of that sunshine, and if I listen carefully, I can hear how this house was filled, too, with the sound of her feet, clipping up the stairs in the morning.

This house is filled with the quiet play of an only child, and, later, it's filled with the never-ending ring of a telephone, once a lifeline for a teenage girl. It's filled with the hushed whispers of my parents' late-night kitchen-table conversations the year they decided to close their business. It's filled with the sound of laughter over Sunday night television, all of us together in the den, watching "MASH" or "Newhart," and it's filled with the soft twang of my mom's accent — the one I have, too — singing, while she sweeps, the forgotten songs of Loretta Lynn and John Denver.

Country roads, take me home.

But through the years, things have changed. Now, this house is no longer in the country. Town has edged in; the place isn't as remote as it once was. There's a grocery store a mile up the road. There are stoplights and heavy tractor-trailers that whiz by at all hours of the day and night.

And so, maybe they're right. Maybe it's time to let go, to find a new space to fill.

This house, which once held promise, now only holds the past. And my parents can take that with them when they go.

Full Circle

WE GOT DROPPED OFF in the gravel parking lot outside Jones Skating Rink, and when our parents drove off for the evening, we took our places outside in the line to get in, shy and awkward and self-conscious, but pretending that we were none of those things.

Some kids carried their own skates, dangling them from the laces over their arms, but most of us had to rent. Scuffed white for the girls; faded black for the boys.

Inside, our eyes adjusted to the dim light and Rod Stewart rasped about young hearts feeling free tonight and everything smelled sugary and sweaty, a heady mixture of Hubba Bubba bubble gum that we packed in our cheeks and Tickle deodorant that we'd just started to use, a requirement of dressing out in P.E. at school.

In between songs, we traded skinny sticks of Juicy Fruit and Fruit Stripe and Doublemint, peeling off the foil and popping the gum in our mouths in case we got pulled onto the floor for a couples' skate, which meant holding hands made sticky by pouring "suicides" — a mixture of Dr Pepper and Coke and Sprite from the soda fountain — and trying not to tangle our feet together when we made the crossover turn.

Learning to skate is not easy, but somehow we managed to figure out how to glide side to side, how to push off with our legs, how to hold on to the rail along the wall, how to hold on to a boy's back pocket, fingers hooked into the slim space next to his comb.

Life is a series of rotations, of revolutions. Cycles and circles.

We did the best we could, trying not to look so shy and awkward and self-conscious, by keeping ourselves moving, going around and around in circles, all of us in unison, some of us learning to skate backward, retrograde, flying around the rink with our knees bent and our necks craned to see if we were going to run into anyone, which we somehow, miraculously, never did, and not once realizing that all life is a series of rotations, of revolutions. Cycles and circles.

I still remember how it feels to skate around that rink, leaning into the curves, and it makes me remember other things, too, like how I cried the first time I rode the Oaken Bucket at Carowinds, a standing ride that suspended you against a wall by centrifugal force as it spun around and around and the bottom dropped away, leaving you with the terrifying feeling that you would plummet to who-knows-where if this ride ever stopped turning, which it most certainly would.

Then, in 1979, *National Geographic* packaged a record inside its pages, a thin flexi-disk that you could tear out and play on a turntable, and I played it — "Songs of the Humpback Whale" — over and over, mesmerized not only by the haunting and lonely sounds of these mammals but also by the record itself, which was an oddly shaped square, but it spun perfectly anyway, around and around, 33⅓ revolutions per minute.

And there were other moments of revolutions that now I recognize as revelations: the lazy Susan in the center of the kitchen table at my grandmother's house that held her W. Dalton china, Serenity pattern; and how my grandmother and I sat at that table and played teatime with her fanciest china, how we spun the lazy Susan, around and around, to turn the creamer or sugar bowl toward each other, and how her entire collection now graces my own china cabinet, plates that I use for everything, even if I'm only grilling a cheeseburger for myself, because she would've said to make every day a special day; and I remember, too, how later, on the porch at her house, we watched the metal canister down in the wooden ice cream freezer turning, going around and around, churning out the first batch of vanilla that we couldn't wait to taste for the first time in the summer, and how afterward she let me race to the backyard where she set up a sprinkler, and I ran around and around in wide circles, barefooted, dodging the streams of water shooting from its rotating base, hearing the *ffpp, ffpp, ffpp, ffpp* of water arcing across the yard while I flailed my outstretched arms, like an octopus, not shy or awkward or self-conscious at all and never considering how much I would miss when this sprinkler stopped turning, which it most certainly would. ◀

Southern Storms

Y GRANDMOTHER ALWAYS KNEW when a storm was coming.

If we had the windows open in the house, or if we were out in the yard digging in her garden, she would smell it first.

"It's going to come up a cloud," she'd say, lifting her chin toward the sky, and she was always right.

Back then, there was no Weather Channel with 24-hour satellite imagery, of course, so people like my grandmother relied on their own senses to tell them whenever a shift was happening in the atmosphere.

I hated storms, especially the fierce ones that popped up in the summer. Deep growls of thunder shook the old windows in her house and terrified me. I kept my eyes closed when the lightning tore at the sky.

Whenever we had one of these storms, I hid on my grandmother's bed with my head buried in her pillow, while she sat on the front porch, rocking. She loved it. It was as though there was just something in her, drawing her to this porch, to the outdoors, while thunder erupted all around and rain slid off the roof in sheets. It was as if she had a front-row seat to a full-scale musical, and

For her, life — its sunny days and its stormy ones, too — was worth the price of admission.

I never questioned her accuracy. She knew exactly how long we had to get the laundry off the line before the rain came; she knew how to count between rumbles of thunder and streaks of lightning to tell how far away a storm was.

Sometimes I think it's a skill we've lost.

Right before one of these summertime storms, my grandmother would hurry to get to the porch, so she could sit and watch it roll in.

Not me.

she wanted to stay for the whole show. My grandmother was like that. She got enjoyment out of everything. For her, life — its sunny days and its stormy ones, too — was worth the price of admission.

Occasionally, when I was feeling brave, I'd inch out from the bedroom and make my way to the screen door, where I could watch her.

I can see her there as clear as if it were yesterday, dressed in one of her polyester pantsuits, her lean legs crossed. My grandmother was both

country and elegant. She knew how to pat out a pan of the best biscuits you've ever had in your life; she knew how to avoid chiggers when she was picking blackberries; and she knew how to drape a strand of pearls around her slender neck and look like the most beautiful woman in the world.

I wanted to sit out there with her, but I just couldn't bring myself to do it. Through the metal grates of the screen door, I'd ask in a tiny voice, "Don't you want to come back in, Grandma?" And

she would because she knew I was scared. She knew how to comfort me, too, her only granddaughter. That was another thing it seemed like she was born knowing how to do.

I miss her so much. I wish I could sit with her now and watch for one of those late-summer storms. But, instead, I can lift my chin to the sky, and listen for the thunder, and wait for the rain.

When it comes, it'll smell so good.

Friday Night Fish Fry

TO GET TO **LITTLE TEXAS FISH CAMP** from my house in Randolph County, you had to cross a one-lane bridge that ran beside a dam. The bridge was past the round of a curve, and it was tricky business to watch for headlights from an approaching car. If one was coming, you'd either gun it to get across first or ease over to the side and wait your turn.

Other fish houses were easier to get to in Asheboro, but in my memory, nothing was better than Little Texas.

On Friday nights, my parents and I went for the all-you-can-eat flounder. Thick strips of fried fish stretched across the whole length of a platter. Hush puppies you could eat like popcorn. Tartar sauce. A pile of slaw, its sweet juice pooling out onto the plate.

I never thought of Little Texas as a "seafood restaurant." To me and everyone else who went there, it was just a fish house, plain and simple, a nondescript, block building set in a dip between two hills next to the Uwharrie River in the middle of the woods, a place with paper placemats on the tables, tiled with squares of ads for appliance or car repair in Denton and real estate sellers in Asheboro.

The place was always packed on weekends with families like mine, and the air hung thick with a mixture of oil from the fryers and cigarette smoke.

You'd carry that smell on your clothes when you left.

At the end of the meal, we'd walk out into the dark Uwharrie night, my dad or grandfather working a toothpick, me twirling a lemon sucker in my mouth.

There was nothing simpler, and nothing more satisfying.

Back then, Little Texas tasted, smelled, and looked like everything I knew of Randolph County, which is to say, everything I knew of North Carolina.

> It was a reminder that all you needed at the end of a good week was a familiar place to go.

It was wood paneling and spindle-back chairs; it was sweet tea in a Styrofoam cup; it was pickup trucks and Chevrolet Camaros pulled into the gravel parking lot; it was the primitiveness of an old, one-lane bridge and the comfort of riding in the back seat of a car at night, watching for headlights to show on the other side and trusting the driver to carry you across safely.

It was
a reminder
that all you needed
at the end of a good
week was a familiar place
to go.

Many of the old fish camps I remember have dwindled. People go to different restaurants now, places where the fish has been shipped in from thousands of miles away. Little Texas has closed, and a two-lane bridge was built beside of the one-lane bridge.

I worry sometimes that the tastes of things I remember are changing.

And then, once in a while, I'm surprised.

Not long ago, I spent a few days in Bogue and Pamlico sounds, in a small fishing boat, with people from the North Carolina Coastal Federation. For two days, we talked about fish. We waded in the sounds. We ate at Riverview Cafe in Sneads Ferry, fried flounder and soft-shell crabs.

And we made a stop at a place called J&B AquaFood, an oyster farm. The owner, Jim Swartzenberg, explained his whole operation. And then he held a fresh oyster in the palm of his hand and slid his pocketknife into the lip of the shell. It popped open, and he offered it to me, my first raw one ever, its liquid shimmering and spilling over the sides.

I took it and tipped it into my mouth, and immediately tasted clusters of salt and sea and waves. Then, in one easy, silky mouthful, it tasted like everything I've ever known, which is to say, it tasted like North Carolina: It was dirt, like the country roads I knew, and metallic, like a cast-iron skillet. It was ocean air and a cool springhouse and a weathered landscape and fish houses and one-lane bridges that carry you straight across the water.

It was a tiny little oyster. Plain and simple.

Miles away from my roots, it tasted like home.

To Everything, a Season

ON THE FIRST **F**RIDAY NIGHT in October — the eve of the Asheboro Fall Festival — about a dozen men from the Randolph Cattlemen's Association hauled their blackened barbecue smokers up a grassy hill across from the courthouse and set them down in a single line.

All the main streets downtown — Fayetteville, Sunset, Worth — were barricaded so that vendors could set up their booths in preparation for the thousands of people coming to the festival the next day.

My grandmother lived right behind the courthouse. When I was a child, on the night before the fall festival, she and I would take a walk after supper and get our own behind-the-scenes glimpse at the preparations.

that would play on the bank steps the next day. I'm sure we weren't supposed to be there, but no one ever noticed us, or if they did, they turned a blind eye to the little girl holding the hand of her 70-year-old grandmother, and they let us have our evening.

My favorite thing about the fall festival was getting a candy apple. It was a treat I couldn't get any other time of the year — an extra-large apple speared on a stick and coated with an inch of bright-red, hard-candy shell. When my grandmother and I walked those streets at night, feeling the first chill of an early-autumn evening on our arms, I'd think about how excited I was to come back the next day and buy my candy apple for 75 cents. It'd take about a half-a-day to finish it. Then, in the afternoon,

It wouldn't be long before the leaves would start to turn and fall from the trees.

We sneaked around, lifting up the capes covering booths with pottery and quilts and peeking underneath. We got to see, before anyone else did, the needlework samplers and silk-screened T-shirts and string art and wooden toys handmade by local craftsmen. We watched the crews set up the stage for the gospel and country-music groups

I'd stand in the line at the Cattlemen's tent for a barbecue sandwich, put together by those men who'd worked all night behind a long table, cutting and chopping meat with their cleavers, slinging mountains of pork into large, aluminum casserole pans, getting it ready for the women to slap into buns, top with slaw, and wrap in wax paper.

Everything had its timetable.

By about 8 p.m., as my grandmother and I were heading back home, we'd start to smell the barbecue from that hill, that perfect marriage of smoke and pork, the air singed with burning wood throwing bits of ash toward the sky. The smokers blazed red, and we'd hear the men on the hill, laughing and talking. They'd stay there all night, tending to their meat and dozing in lawn chairs, waking early to spike it with vinegar and sauce and get it all chopped up and ready for Saturday's crowd.

I loved the festival, but even more, I loved the night before, when it was just the two of us, my grandmother and me, enjoying our own private prelude to fall.

Back then, it seemed like there'd be plenty more quiet autumn evenings to experience, plenty more brilliant-blue autumn skies to enjoy the next day.

I didn't realize then that it wouldn't be long before the leaves would start to turn and fall from the trees.

It wouldn't be long before I wouldn't walk these streets with my grandmother anymore.

It wouldn't be long before another season would come and go.

At the time, I didn't think about those kinds of things. And if my grandmother did, she didn't let on. We lived in the moment, she and I. We walked home in the shadow of an autumn moon, shuffling amid the maples and birch leaves that had started to scatter on the sidewalk, watching a new season unfold right at our feet. ◀

Fall Back

FOR 17 DAYS IN AUTUMN, I sat in the waiting room of the surgical ICU at Moses Cone Hospital in Greensboro while my dad lay in a hospital bed, intubated with a ventilator, a machine breathing for him.

It was a horrible thing to see, my dad swollen with the 20 extra pounds of fluid that surgery pumped in. A medusa of tubes. Machines rigged to his body. He had surgery for a diseased lung on a Tuesday, then another surgery for a blood clot on Wednesday. Twelve days after that, the doctors shocked his heart to correct its irregular rhythm. Then, pneumonia. Just as he started to recover from one thing, something else happened to set him back.

Every day, my mom drove from Asheboro to sit by his bedside. She woke up every morning at 5 a.m., showered, drove the dark highway before the sun came up, and stayed at the hospital until visiting hours ended at 7 p.m.

Clocks are everywhere in the hospital. In my dad's room on the second floor, a clock was behind the bed, and a clock was in front of the bed. The hospital has 518 patient beds, and each room has at least one clock; many have two. Clocks hang outside each room, too, and on every hall. Clocks are in the half-dozen central waiting rooms. Clocks are in the 16 operating rooms.

I don't know why there are so many clocks. Anyone who's been in a hospital knows that time stands still.

> I'm grateful for the smallest things that can make the days easier, that give a little relief.

Here, everyone is watching a clock, waiting for something. Waiting for news. Waiting for a doctor. Waiting for recovery.

They told my dad, "It's just going to take time."

This year, daylight saving time ends on November 6, and all those clocks, the ones beside the 518 beds, the ones in the rooms, in the hallways, in the waiting areas, will automatically adjust back an hour.

Reverting back to standard time in the fall moves an hour of sunlight from the evening to the morning. It means that if my mom is still driving to the hospital each morning, she won't be in the dark.

This November, a time of thanksgiving, I'm grateful for the smallest things that can make the days easier, that give a little relief. Sunlight in the morning. Clear autumn skies. Hot coffee from a vending machine. Casseroles packed in Tupperware. Strangers who care for people they don't even know.

On day 17 in the hospital, when I walked into my dad's room, he had his eyes open. I've noticed how much my own dark eyes look just like his. He still had his ventilator, and he couldn't talk, but he was holding a pen and scrawling notes on a piece of paper: "My throat hurts." "I wish I could have some water." "Nose itches."

I watched my mom rub her thumb across my dad's nose. A small thing. A little relief.

On day 17, my mom and I were leaving the critical care ward for the evening. My dad lifted his hands, reaching for us. My mom held onto one of his hands; I held onto the other. The nurse stood in the doorway and watched us. "What a sweet family," she said.

My dad squeezed our fingers tight, closed his eyes and nodded. I felt the wave of peace wash over the three of us.

And time stood still.

Christmas Magic

CHRISTMAS CAME TO MY HOUSE on December 1, the day my mom hung the Advent calendar on the closet door in the hallway. For the next 24 days, I unwrapped the tiny presents that appeared in the little pockets.

The calendar was silk-screen linen, handmade in Denmark. It had 24 small pockets sewn onto the front, beneath a screen-printed image of children circling a Christmas tree.

Every morning when I got up, still in my pajamas, my mom and I walked together to check the Advent calendar, and there would be a new toy, folded neatly inside a Kleenex or wrapped in a tiny piece of brown wrapping paper, peeking out from one of the pockets. I can still remember how excited I got by all this, seeing a toy popping up from one of those pockets, as if it had appeared there by magic.

After work at night, my mom stopped at the Quik Chek on her way home and bought toys from the vending machine in the doorway. She stuffed the pockets of the Advent calendar with all kinds of things: plastic ring whistles, squares of Bazooka Joe gum, a rubber high-bounce ball, and ceramic animal figurines — a duck, a cow, a frog — each one about the size of a penny.

One year, each pocket held a different pewter miniature. There was a candlestick collection, each one about half the size of a toothpick. I got a tiny set of pewter dishes — four plates and four cups. A pewter iron. A pewter mirror, brush, and comb. A pewter fireplace shovel and stoker.

On Christmas Day that year, I woke up to find a dollhouse beneath our tree. It was beautiful — a two-story, white, wooden farmhouse — and it was electrified. Each room had tiny sconces mounted on the walls, and when the lights were lit, the whole house glowed.

My parents gave me the best childhood Christmases.

The front facade of the house was on hinges, and you could swing the entire piece forward to get to the rooms inside. There was a living room and kitchen, a staircase, two bedrooms, two bathrooms. There was a fireplace, and I jumped up to get the candlestick set from my Advent calendar and placed it inside on the mantel. Such a tiny thing that filled in the empty space. It made the house seem complete.

The dollhouse was one of the best Christmas presents I ever got, and I spent hours stretched out on the

floor in front of it, arranging furniture, imagining scenarios inside it, creating stories for its little people.

Years later, my parents told me about driving to Davidson to buy that dollhouse. They found a craftsman who had a shop across the street from Davidson College, and they went to look at what he had. I can imagine the two of them walking on the sidewalk at Christmastime, admiring the decorations, stopping at The Soda Shop for a hot dog lunch, and looking in all the store windows for Christmas presents for their little girl. I can imagine how excited my mom must have been seeing that house on display in the shop window, its front opened up to a miniature, happy home that reminded her of our own. I can imagine the smile spreading across my dad's face when he loaded that house up in the truck bed, wrapping a blanket around the structure so it wouldn't get damaged on the drive back home.

My parents gave me the best childhood Christmases.

I guess that wasn't magic at all.

January Snow

N **JANUARY 25, 2000,** about 13 inches of snow fell at my home in Greensboro.

Raleigh got a foot and a half — it beat the record for 17.8 inches set in 1927. Siler City got 22 inches, and in some areas of the state, more than two feet fell.

The Federal Emergency Management Association called it "the most powerful winter storm to hit North Carolina in 72 years."

The forecast the night before predicted a dusting to less than an inch. This storm caught everyone by surprise.

My dad, at home in Randolph County, woke up at 3 a.m. Because of the brightness reflecting into the house, he thought it was morning. He got up, and went into the kitchen for coffee, but the coffeemaker hadn't brewed. He noticed it was cold in the house. He noticed that it was unusually quiet. Cars that normally whizzed down Old Highway 49 were absent.

And then he looked outside.

My parents' den is sunken, and the windows look out at ground level. The snow rose halfway up the windows and stood shin-high in front of the doors. For a moment, my dad — trapped in a house buried in so much snow, by Randolph County standards anyway, he could barely push the back door open — thought surely this was the end of the world. He'd never seen anything like it.

The weight of the snow pulled down power lines and trees; more than a quarter of a million people in North Carolina lost power for a week.

was on the ground.

That's the thing about snow. It dulls most of the senses. It muffles sound, mutes smell. It's numbing to touch. It masks the landscape with whiteness, rendering everything colorless.

In artist terms, white is the absence of color. But in reality, it's just the opposite; it's the culmination of all colors, the swirling together of everything in the light spectrum.

Some people look at snow and see all of its pitfalls: its potential for destruction, its hazards and dangers, its ability to bring small towns to their

It was hard not to be transfixed by the beauty of what was on the ground.

Towns shut down. Power crews worked round the clock. My parents lit candles and boiled coffee on the top of their kerosene heater, and they did the only thing they could do: They waited for the sun. They waited for the sun to come out and make it all go away.

And yet, at night, despite the cold and the lack of power and the crack of branches breaking through the silence, when the moon cast its glimmer across my parents' front yard, it was hard not to be transfixed by the beauty of what

knees. Some people look at snow and see all its beauty and how it covers all the imperfections in a landscape.

Careful observers see both sides. Nature carries with it the power for calamity and the opportunity for calm.

It's the culmination — the swirling together of everything, the wild and the tame, the light and the dark — that makes it all so beautiful.

From Scratch

SATURDAY MORNING, nearly 40 years ago, and here's what's on the kitchen table at my grandmother's house: six eggs and two sticks of butter warming to room temperature, a box of Swans Down flour, a metal measuring bowl full of sugar, a tiny bottle of vanilla extract.

My grandmother made her pound cakes on Saturdays, and I loved watching her work. By themselves, the ingredients on the table were nothing special, but in my grandmother's hands, they transformed into something magnificent.

I was mesmerized by the steps: how she smeared butter with her fingertips into the bottom of the pans; how she sprinkled flour on the pans and tilted them to

knock it loose; how she cracked eggs with two fingers and measured milk by holding the glass cup up to eye level to see the faded line marker; how she scraped the sides of the mixing bowl and then passed me the spatula to lick.

So many things can go wrong with a cake. Too dry. Sticks to the pan. Crumbly. Sinks in the middle. Domes on top. But my grandmother's, somehow, were always perfect.

If cooking is an imprecise art and baking is a science, then cakes, surely, are one level deeper. Chemistry.

All the elements — ordinary ingredients by themselves — must come together in such a precise way to create the right reaction.

My grandmother knew to alternate dry and wet ingredients — first flour, then milk, then flour — but she probably didn't know the chemical reasons why it must be this way. (Otherwise, too much protein gluten forms and makes the cake tough.)

Mix — not too much, not too little — and then carefully slide into the oven. For the next 50 minutes, I'd sit at the table and color quietly, dangling my feet and trying not to move around too much, for fear of causing the cake to fall. Cakes, by their nature, are fragile. They require tenderness. Patience. And care.

A cake is simultaneously refined and down-home.

Thinking back, it was a complicated process that took about two hours, start to finish.

I guess it's that precise process that gives cakes their character, that makes a cake what it is. Something special.

A cake is simultaneously refined and down-home, and by its very construction, it towers above all other desserts. It's no wonder we put them on pedestals.

And it's why cakes — more than cookies, more than pies, more than puddings or cobblers — are the ultimate expression of love and celebration. Cakes mark special occasions. Birthdays, anniversaries, weddings, grand events.

My grandmother made a cake nearly every Saturday. For her, all of life was a special occasion.

In our own expression of love for North Carolina, we created five original cakes that, to our knowledge, don't exist anywhere outside the pages of this magazine. For months, we worked with a recipe developer and baker to create our versions of North Carolina cakes, using nearly all local ingredients and recalling flavors that give us North Carolinians our character, too: pimento cheese, country ham, Krispy Kreme doughnuts, Nabs, Pepsi and peanuts.

A little unexpected, maybe, but that's the other beautiful thing about cakes. Even when you're expecting them, they always seem to surprise.

I remember how my grandmother made her cakes nearly 40 years ago. The process, for anyone who cares to take it on, is still the same. Slow. Deliberate.

But the result is always a masterpiece.

This Road

OUTSIDE THE SOUTHWEST CITY LIMITS of Asheboro, N.C. Highway 49 — a connector between Raleigh and Charlotte — splits. Veer off to the right, past the old Yates Country Ham building and the Asheboro Animal Hospital, and you're traveling on Old N.C. Highway 49.

It's a nice drive. Old 49 is still a quiet, country road with plain-built houses and pine trees, and open fields spotted with baled hay and horses. About a mile into the drive, you see the gentle rise of the Uwharries. I grew up on this road, in a house on a hill.

After I got my driver's license, I burned up this road and all its offshoots. I drove it back and forth to school, high school first, then later, when I went west to Appalachian State University. On weekend nights, I shuttled my friends from Farmer and Denton and Jackson Creek, all of us piling into my car to go to town and drive some more.

Back then, everyone in the country went to the city to cruise Fayetteville Street. "Town," as we called Asheboro proper, was a good 20-minute drive from wherever you happened to be on Old Highway 49.

When we got to town, we followed the cruising etiquette established decades before we got to this road: Start out on the south end and fall into the line of traffic, a teenage-led procession of Camaros and Mustangs and pickup trucks. Drive north, past Hardee's, past the bowling alley on the hill, past Sir Pizza, past McDonald's, to the shopping center anchored by Roses', then loop around in the parking lot and start all over. The point of cruising was to keep moving.

At the end of an evening cruising, I took my friends home, back down Old 49 toward Farmer and Denton and Jackson Creek. I had this road all to myself again.

You saw only the road, a black asphalt river stretching in front of the car.

I loved driving Old 49 at night. The periphery disappeared into the darkness. You didn't see the trees anymore, or the power lines, or the fields or the houses. You saw only the road, a black asphalt river stretching in front of the car no farther than headlights and the stars overhead allowed. The shortened sight distance made driving intimate; it connected you to the road in a way that driving in the daytime can't, where there are other distractions, other

things to pull your attention away from what is laid out right in front of you.

It's funny how you get to know something so well that you know every detail about it. I've driven Old 49 so often in my life, I could navigate it blindfolded. I know its smooth, straight stretches and its ruts and how much to ease off the gas around its sharpest turns. I know where to watch for deer that could come bounding out of the darkness.

One day, I know I won't drive this road anymore.

My friends all live elsewhere now, and when the day comes and my parents are gone, there'll be no reason for me to come back.

There's talk of a major highway coming through a hundred yards from my parents' house, bisecting Old 49 at the top of the hill. That'll surely change the road I know. We have more than 100,000 miles of public roads in North Carolina, with more constructed each year. It's a good thing, I suppose. It keeps us moving. There are places I remember that don't exist anymore, places that have been completely rerouted. U.S. Highway 220 South going to Asheboro has expanded. There's a lake under the bridge at Randleman. So many of the old roads I knew are different now.

At night in the dark, though, they still look the same, black asphalt rivers that stretch endlessly into a distance that you can't see.

Flowers in the Sky

TEN YEARS **AGO,** when my dad retired, he went to Tractor Supply in Asheboro and Southside Hardware in High Point and bought the following:

One dozen 55-gallon galvanized, metal trash cans; four 30-gallon galvanized, metal trash cans; two 18-gallon galvanized, metal trash cans; and two oval washtubs.

After he hauled all these trash cans home, he drilled holes in the bottom of each one and set them in a 30-by-40-foot area to the side of the house. He filled each trash can with empty two-liter Ginger Ale bottles to take up space and make the cans lighter and easier to move around. Then he poured in bags of potting soil. Not a lot; just enough dirt for roots to burrow.

Then he added his plants.

My dad, who was never a gardener, planted morning glories and nasturtiums, sweet peas and bluebonnets. He planted herbs in the smaller cans: rosemary and basil and thyme for their green color. He planted vegetables, too: tomatoes and squash and eggplant and peppers. He planted sunflowers and trumpet vines in the waist-high cans, staking them so they towered high.

grocery store stopped my parents and said, "Y'all are the ones who live in the house with the tin-can garden."

All those years in that house and my parents never had a garden. Not even a flower bed. For 30 years, they worked long hours running their business, leaving the house every day, even on the weekends, early in the morning, coming home well after dark. There was no time to put flowers in the ground.

> My dad called to my mom to come out and see the moonflower, shimmering white against a black, country sky.

And he planted moonflowers, their big, beautiful blooms coming out only at night. In the evening, after supper, my dad called to my mom to come out and see the moonflower, shimmering white against a black, country sky.

It all was a sight to see. People stopped on the back road behind my parents' house and walked down the hill into the yard to see what was growing. They were curious about these plants that popped out of those metal trash cans, plants that grew seven and eight feet high. People in the

The earth around my parents' house was too poor, too full of rocks and red clay to properly dig up for a garden, and my dad, who was never a gardener, didn't have the right tools anyhow for preparing a traditional plot. So he improvised. He thought of something different.

He wanted a garden.

Instead of putting one in the ground, he put one in the sky. ◄

Places Like This

YOU KNOW WHAT KIND OF PLACE THIS IS. You can tell by the information rack in the doorway, bulging with real estate guidebooks and Auto Weekly newspapers. A metal "Seat yourself" sign points you to the interior of the restaurant. A drape of fishnets hangs from the brown-paneled back wall, above a framed picture of a trawler.

Over a row of booths, an old clock swings its pendulum, looking as if it's been in place for 30, 40, maybe 50 years or more, and behind the cash register, a "new" electric Pepsi clock marks time in shifts — early lunch, lunch, late lunch. Early dinner, dinner.

There is no late dinner in places like this.

Wall-mounted phones still ring. People call to place take-out orders or to check hours. Cashiers say, "We close at 10."

In places like this, you can sit anywhere you like. A waitress wearing sneakers brings sweet tea to your table in 16-ounce Styrofoam cups, lemon wedges partially submerged in the crunchy pellet ice. After she sets the drinks down, she tilts her hip upward to get to the straws tucked in her apron pocket, then fans them out like she's dealing cards. In tandem, everyone at the table reaches for a straw and tamps it down to break its paper seal.

You already know what you want in a place like this: the combination platter. Fried flounder and oysters or Calabash-style shrimp, hush puppies, and French fries. Sometimes you might substitute a baked potato. Snow crab legs. Scallops.

A mound of coleslaw.

And more tea, please.

In places like this, waitresses raise trays high overhead and maneuver the dining room with a dancer's grace.

The food is only one reason we come to places like this.

They refill the industrial tea brewers — Luzianne five-gallon barrels — constantly, and they shuffle pots on the four-burner Bunn coffeemaker like they're playing the shell game; here go two with orange rims to denote decaf, here go two with black rims to denote regular.

They shovel ice from the 900-pound Scotsman cooler, a whale of an ice machine, into pitchers, and they pull plates of food from beneath the metal heat lamps in the kitchen. Everyone moves and dodges, bobs and weaves, swimming with the constant current of a busy eastern North Carolina seafood restaurant.

In places like this, children sit backward in booths with their parents. They hold onto to the top edge of the seat and crouch down, then peer over, eyeing diners at the next table. They fidget and squirm and wiggle like fish until the parents give a look and tell the child to sit.

In places like this, the children sit.

In places like this, the men in the kitchen wear T-shirts and tans and full-body aprons that loop around their necks. Young men who come in to eat with their young families wear sunglasses on top of their heads. Old men come in with gold watches and hairy forearms and wedding bands that look as if they've been in place for 30, 40, maybe 50 years or more. And there's always a military guy — you can tell by his high-and-tight haircut and the respectful way he says "Yes, ma'am," to the waitress when she asks if he needs more tea. He sits with his girlfriend or wife and child, and you remember that you're in a place within short driving distance of eight significant military bases. You nod to him when you walk out.

And when you walk out, you tug on your belt loop to pull your pants up a little, and you rare back, belly tight as a tick. In places like this, you always eat too much. You pay and amble back to the table, which has been cleared by now, and drop a stack of ones and a five. It's a good tip.

The food is only one reason we come to places like this.

We come to these places — the Sanitary Fish Market in Morehead City, Owens' in Nags Head, the Provision Company in Southport, Fisherman's Wharf in Wanchese, and hundreds more in between — because we know what we want, and we know what we're going to get. And when we come in straight off the beach, our skin still warm from the sun, our legs crusted with salt, we know we're welcome here.

You know what kind of place this is. This is our kind of place.

Larger Than Life

N **1982, THE TAR HEELS WON** the NCAA championship.

I sat in the den with my dad and watched the game with him on a Magnavox television that weighed more than I did. I didn't know anything about basketball, except that all the players wore tiny shorts and tube socks that went up to their knees.

It was a rare occasion when my dad had the night off from work, and the two of us sat on the couch together, watching players whose names I didn't know run back and forth.

I tried to stay interested. Then, at the end of the game, Michael Jordan launched his winning shot. My dad, who is normally reserved, jumped up, a cigarette in the corner of his mouth, and started chanting the fight song — rah, rah, Car'lina-lina! He grabbed me, and I jumped up, too, both of us spinning around in the den, listening to the words "North Carolina! North Carolina!" come out of the TV, over and over.

The next day, everyone at Farmer School, where I was in the sixth grade, went crazy. For some reason, back then, we all identified with one of two teams: State or Carolina. Probably not a one of us had ever been to Raleigh or Chapel Hill — and I know none of us had ever heard of, say, Wake Forest — but that didn't matter. All year long, we paraded down the halls in our Carolina blue ankle socks and our cherry-red Wolfpack T-shirts, and we traced the schools' logos on the fronts of our spiral notebooks.

The day after Carolina won, the principal at Farmer School played the fight song — rah, rah, Car'lina-lina — over the intercom. We cheered from our classroom seats. A few days later, Carolina Canners came out with grape-flavored Carolina Blue Soda. It was in a blue can, and the drink inside was blue, too, and everyone at my school — even the State fans — walked across the field to Farmer Store at lunchtime to buy one.

> It gave us something larger to connect to, something that went beyond the borders of our own county.

For people like me, growing up in a rural county without a university or even a big city nearby, that game catapulted basketball into something more than just basketball. It gave us something larger to connect to, something that went beyond the borders of our own county. As kids, we identified with larger-than-life symbols, like basketball players who made memorable jump shots.

Looking back, I realize we

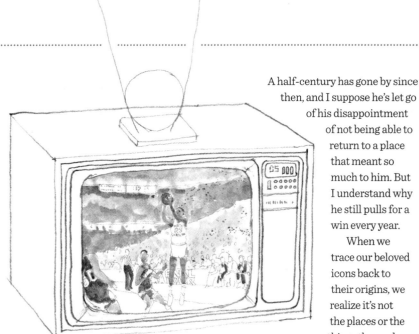

A half-century has gone by since then, and I suppose he's let go of his disappointment of not being able to return to a place that meant so much to him. But I understand why he still pulls for a win every year.

When we trace our beloved icons back to their origins, we realize it's not the places or the things themselves that are important; it's the memories they represent. As much as we love our lighthouses, our barbecue, our basketball, something else matters more.

It's those summers spent in the shadow of Cape Hatteras, when both of our grandparents were still living. It's the chicken biscuit from Biscuitville on the way home after church and the bottle of Cheerwine opened at the end of a long day working outside. It's our mother's sweet voice singing softly to Doc Watson's "Keep on the Sunny Side," when she thought no one was listening.

And it's the basketball game that we watched for the first time with our dad, the one that made him — and us, too — stand up and cheer.

claimed our allegiance blindly. There was no particular reason for us, at age 12, to be State fans or Carolina fans, except that we watched our parents, who taught us how to be.

My dad stood up and cheered for UNC's win that night because he went to school there. I remember the story he told me about hitchhiking from Asheboro to Chapel Hill. He didn't have a car, and he didn't have any other means of getting there. He went to UNC for two years and fell in love with it. Just before his third year, he found out that my grandparents didn't have enough money to send him back. He had to quit and go to work.

Where Hospitality Lives

MY GREAT-GRANDMOTHER, Jessie Mabel Coble — "Granny" to my mother — lived in a two-story wooden farmhouse out in the country in Julian. The siding on the house wasn't painted, and the front porch didn't have any underpinnings. Chickens ran around beneath the house.

There was no heat, except for a woodstove in the kitchen. Jessie Mabel's husband, Henry Pat — "Papaw," to my mother — got up at 3 a.m. every day to light the woodstove for heat and so Granny could cook.

There was no running water in the house. No indoor plumbing. They got their water from the well house, and drank it, ice cold, right out of the dipper. A washtub stayed outside, and they filled it for their baths in the evening.

Jessie Mabel — Granny — was country. No one ever taught her proper manners or etiquette. She dipped snuff in the day and sat on the front porch of an evening with a broken-off hickory stick between her fingers, peeled back the bark, and cleaned her teeth. She sat like a man, with her legs apart. She reached for things across the table. She never wrote a single thank-you note.

But Jessie Mabel Coble set pitchers of tea for the 15 or so tobacco hands who came inside for lunch. And she kept food on the table all the time: fried chicken and bowls of cucumber and onions in vinegar and pickled beets and potatoes and corn and homemade biscuits — all this beneath a tablecloth to shield the food from flies.

My mother loved it at Granny's house, a place with no running water and no heat and where the food had to be covered up. Because for everything it didn't have, here's what it did have: It was warm. It was friendly. It was comfortable.

> She knew it was important to share her resources, as limited as they were.

In the mornings, Granny sat with my mother on the front porch, the two of them side by side in old cane-bottom chairs. They shelled butter beans and churned buttermilk. She taught my mom how to pour butter into wooden butter molds and how to tap it out so that the pretty leaf pattern showed up on top. You wanted your butter to look nice, not for company, because company rarely came, but simply because it looked nice.

In the evenings, Granny brushed

my mother's hair, long, slow strokes over and over, smoothing out her thick strands and checking for ticks.

It felt good to have someone care about you like that. To have someone give you that kind of attention.

When Hurricane Hazel hit in 1954, my mother was at Granny's house. They were terrified of the wind and the rain. They hid beneath a quilt on top of Granny's iron bed, and when they heard the hickory tree fall on the well house, they held on to each other, waiting for the storm to pass.

Many years later, after I was born, my mother drove out to the country to pick up Granny and brought her home to stay at our house for a week. The two of them made a quilt, a Grandma's Flower Garden pattern. My mother still has this quilt — it covers the iron bed, Granny's bed, in my parents' house — and you can tell whose stitches are whose: My mother's are precise and even; Granny's

are longer and a little more ragged. Both are beautiful.

Jessie Mabel Coble couldn't have told you what Southern hospitality is. She didn't know to bring a covered dish to a church supper — in fact, she didn't even go to church, although she carried thankfulness in her heart. But she knew it was important to share her resources, as limited as they were. And she knew that it was important to give her time, her care, and, especially, her comfort to a little girl.

Southern hospitality isn't always fancy. Sometimes, it's unadorned. It doesn't always need white linens and porcelain teacups. It doesn't always remove its hat.

It just needs a place where people, when they come there, feel at home.

A Place to Walk

WHERE I GREW UP, there wasn't anywhere to go for a walk. I didn't live in a neighborhood; I lived in the country. There were no sidewalks, and you wouldn't want to walk along the side of the road, in the taller grass and weeds, where there might be snakes.

Cars drive fast on country roads. Teenage boys sometimes throw things out the windows.

So I'd drive into town to walk at the lighted high school track or at the Oak Lawn Cemetery across from the Energizer Battery plant. A paved path looped around the grounds there, and it was a good, safe place to walk.

Where I live now, there are sidewalks. I go out every evening after supper. You can mark time by how things on the street change with the seasons.

In the summer, I walk toward a big magnolia at the end of the street. The branches hang low, and in July, when the blooms are as big as baseballs, I put my face right in them and breathe in their soft scent. In August, the crape myrtles scatter pink blossoms all over the ground, and in winter, the same pattern shows up in snowfall.

Sometimes, when I'm with them, I catch myself walking too fast, moving ahead.

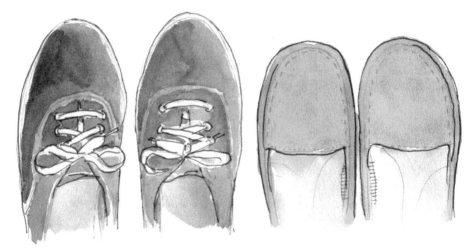

On Sunday evenings, trash bins line the curbs. It's interesting what people throw away. Families have a lot of trash; people who live alone have a lot less.

On my route the other night, I passed an old woman who was coming out of the front door of her house.

She carried a single white trash bag, taking it to her trash bin. Didn't look like she had much in it. I made an entire loop of the street before she made it to her trash can.

She called out to me. "Boy, you're fast," she said. And then, "I used to walk fast like that."

It made me slow down.

It made me think about how the people whom I love walk. I think about how my grandmother walked so much when I was little; in the afternoons, she and I walked so many of the streets in downtown Asheboro, stopping to visit neighbors who wanted to show us their gardens or have us sit on their porches with them or have us listen to them play the piano and eat a piece of pie. I wanted to keep walking — that's what we were out there to do, I thought — but I know now those neighbors were lonely. Now I know we weren't just walking.

By the time my grandmother was 80, she still wanted to walk, but she needed me to hold to. I tried, but I'm not sure I did a very good job. I was so much younger. And impatient.

I think about my mom, about how years of working and standing on unforgiving concrete left her legs covered in horrible varicose veins; my dad, too. The two of them walk slowly now. My dad shuffles in his leather loafers. My mom takes small steps. They hold on to each other.

Sometimes, when I'm with them, I catch myself walking too fast, moving ahead. I look behind me, and I see their faces, smiling and struggling a little to catch up. I'm learning how to stop and wait. I'm learning how to hold out my arm, to give them something to hold on to.

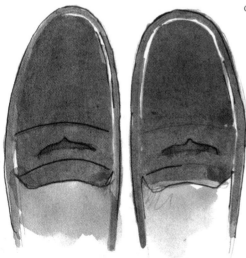

What Our Soil Holds

THE SOIL IN NORTH CAROLINA makes me think of the dust kicked up by the school bus that sped down the dirt road behind my parents' house after it dropped me off on those cool, fall days.

I watched the bus go down the road, trailing an orange smoke screen, and I stuck to the ditch until the dirt cloud settled and I could walk on the road again. I breathed through my nose, but I still managed to taste the dry powder of dirt, of iron-rich Piedmont soil in my mouth, bitter and metallic.

The soil in North Carolina makes me think of tube baseball socks, mostly white but streaked with an impenetrable stain of red clay. It makes me think of the dirt clods in the Randolph County fields after a tractor has run through, and it makes me think of caked mud striping the sides of the Ford trucks and Camaros in the parking lot of my high school, the result of driving too fast down a dirt-covered country road, windows down and an arm crooked out the side holding on to the roof.

The soil in North Carolina makes me remember my grandmother's fingernails after she dug in her flower garden and how her canvas shoes were always spattered with dirt. She was careful to brush off her pants leg before she came inside, but if I leaned toward her and inhaled, I could smell fresh grass and wood ashes.

> Why, I wonder, do we have such an urge to dig, to excavate, to unearth what is beneath us?

The soil in North Carolina is so potent that, in 1900, scientist Milton Whitney, conducting the state's first soil survey, claimed to be able to identify what type of soil tobacco was grown in just by smelling its smoke.

The soil in North Carolina is a repository. It holds smells and tastes and memories. And more. It holds our agriculture — our potatoes and cotton, our tobacco and corn, our peanuts and soybeans; it holds our earthworms for fishing, our blueberry bushes and strawberry patches, our peach trees and muscadine vines. It holds our gold and our silver and our platinum in ancient alluvial deposits.

When I was a child, I sat at the edge of the stream in our woods and panned for gold with an old aluminum pie tin, dipping it into the muddy water and tilting out the sediment the way I learned to do during a field trip to Reed Gold Mine.

I swished the soil around, and sometimes I caught sight of something sparkling. But I could never grab hold of whatever it was.

When I got tired of doing that, I jabbed at the earth with a stick, dislodging shards of quartz. I spent hours uprooting the earth.

Why, I wonder, do we have such an urge to dig, to excavate, to unearth what is beneath us, to exhume whatever lies under the surface? Why do we attach ourselves so strongly to the ground, to our soil, to our muck and peat, our swamp and marsh, our silt loam, our red clay?

Farmers know the answer. They plow and till and dig and turn over the soil each season, driven to extract from the land those things that sustain our lives. Small wonder, then, that we want to get our hands in it.

And so we keep on. We farm. We garden. We shovel sand at the beach and dig for crabs at sunset. We dig for fossils, for prehistoric sharks' teeth, for Indian arrowheads. We plant a seed half an inch in the soil, and in return, we get something back.

The Blessing of Memory

MY COUSIN STEVE CALLED ME "THE KID." I was two years old, and he was a teenager, and whenever we were in the same place — during holidays at my grandmother's house — Steve swaggered in, all high-school cool, and grinned at my mom. "Where's the kid?" he asked every time.

I don't remember Steve at all. I've seen pictures in old family photo albums, and he looked like the rest of the Hudson family. Jet black hair. A bright smile. Mischievous eyes. I've seen pictures of him holding me, a young guy in bell-bottom jeans, his hair to his collar, swinging a happy little girl in the air.

Steve died in a deer-hunting accident, right around Thanksgiving, 40 years ago.

It knocked my family down.

That year, my parents had already bought Steve's Christmas present, a board game that they thought he'd love. It was already wrapped when everyone got the news.

For years I wondered how anyone was able to unwrap that present. I wondered how anyone was able to eat for months. I wondered how anyone was able to do anything at all.

I don't remember Steve, but now, every year at Thanksgiving, when the weather turns cool and I can smell wood smoke drifting outside, I think about him.

I think about being at my grandmother's house at later Thanksgivings, when Steve's mother, my aunt Joan, told the story about how Steve played Oliver in a play at Trinity High School. At his funeral, someone sang a song from the show.

For years I wondered how she was able to tell this story without crying, but eventually, she did.

It takes a long time before sad memories give way to happier ones.

Somehow, people do.

I think about being at my grandmother's house, when, in the face of the worst thing that could happen to a parent, family gathered.

I think about my grandmother's table, the one that held dinner when Steve died, the one that held dinner *to Steve with love*

when my grandfather died, the one that held dinner when we all came, year after year, cousins and aunts and uncles, and we squeezed together on couches and watched someone fiddle with the antenna on the television while we waited for the football game to come on and then, sliding off the couch and sneaking into the kitchen, we lifted the tinfoil on the sheet pans set out on top of the stove, and we cut tiny squares of my grandmother's Thanksgiving dressing when nobody was looking, eating small pieces in secret and cradling the crumbs in cupped hands beneath our mouths before we wiped our hands off on our pants legs and crawled back up on the couch, sliding in next to each other. Cousins and aunts and uncles.

It takes a long time before sad memories give way to happier ones.

But mercifully — thankfully — somehow this is exactly what happens.

The other day, I asked my dad to tell me about his nephew Steve, the one everyone called Stevie. "Oh," my dad said, "whenever he'd see you, his face would light up. And the first thing he'd say was, 'Where's the kid?'"

I watched my dad as he smiled then, and remembered.

Snow Cream, Simply

NCE, **BEFORE THERE WERE 24-HOUR** weather channels and everything got so fancy, there was simply Frank Deal, weatherman, on Channel 8.

He gave his nightly forecasts standing in front of what looked like a homemade map. He moved around stick-on clouds and arrows to indicate fronts and weather changes. He told corny jokes and read weather facts from a plain-cover book. He threw paper snowflakes in the air whenever there was a chance of snow.

We trusted whatever Frank Deal said. And if he said it was going to snow, my parents parked their cars at the bottom of the driveway, and my grandmother set out her snow-day provisions: A large, stainless-steel mixing bowl. A big serving spoon for scooping snow. A bag of Dixie Crystals. A bottle of McCormick's vanilla extract.

Once, before there were 24-hour supermarkets and everything got so fancy, there were simply small grocery stores that sold limited selections, like just one brand of sugar or whole milk. When Frank Deal said it was going to snow, we went to the store to get an extra gallon of milk to go with our sugar and our vanilla.

Overnight, Frank Deal's predictions, simple but accurate, came true, and we woke up to half an inch of snow or maybe a few inches, or, a real treat, much more.

I liked playing in the snow, but one of the downsides to being an only child was that I didn't have anyone to play with. So my grandmother, sensitive to this, pulled on her wool winter coat and her leather Isotoners and wrapped a scarf around her head and set out for the yard with me.

"All right, let's go inside and make some snow cream."

She taught me how to lie on my back and swing my arms and legs to make a snow angel. She watched me pile snow into a fort. She took clothes from her own closet — pillbox hats and old vinyl purses and clunky pumps — and showed me how to dress the snowman I cobbled together, turning him into a snow woman.

I now know how chilled to the bone she must have been to keep me company in the frozen outdoors. I wouldn't have noticed then, but I remember how she took tentative steps down the back stairs, how she held tight to the icy railing to keep from losing her footing. I remember how she braced herself against a tree, ignoring her own dizzy spells to toss snowballs at my fort. I

remember how she lugged a 10-pound bag of birdseed to the snow-covered feeders, knocking the snow off their roofs with the back of her brittle, arthritic hands. She identified with the creatures for whom winter was a strain.

My grandmother stayed outside with me far longer than she should have, and when my cheeks finally blazed pink and my black hair hung in wet strands across my neck, she'd smile and say, "All right, let's go inside and make some snow cream."

That was my signal to get the bowl and scrape the top layer of untouched snow off whatever flat surface I could find. I piled the bowl as high as I could get it, and we went inside, both of us thawing out in her kitchen as she set to work, whisking milk and sugar and vanilla with the snow.

When the consistency was perfect, she scooped out a mound of snow cream into a cereal bowl for me and got one for herself, too, and we'd eat fast before it all melted, turning our bowls up and drinking the sweet liquid, both of us settling into a silence, a sweet stillness, that I've never had with anyone, not before or since. This was winter, made warm.

Once, before there were hundreds of flavors of ice cream and everything got so fancy, we kept butter pecan and chocolate and Neapolitan on hand in the freezer. But on snow days, we got to make something special, something that you couldn't buy in a store, not then, and really not now, not the same anyway.

Once, before I grew up, there was simply my grandmother and me. And there were winters in which snow came from the sky, simply, as it's done forever and ever without changing, without being different, without any sort of fanciness to it all.

Listening: A Love Story

N THE LATE **1960s,** a woman named Susie — my mother before she was my mother — worked as a waitress at the Sheraton Hotel in Greensboro. She sparkled with personality, and before long, the management promoted her to hostess of the fine-dining restaurant. People came to eat on the nights she was working, and when her regular customers came in the door, she grabbed menus and escorted couples to their special tables.

Not long into her job as hostess, the management moved her again, this time to behind the bar of the Matador Room.

One evening, a man named Phil — my dad before he was my dad — came into the restaurant, sat at the bar, and ordered a Schlitz on draft. My mother poured the drink and thought he was the best-looking man she'd ever seen. He had wavy black hair and a brilliant smile, and she thought he looked just like Joe Namath.

The man, who was my dad before he was my dad, drank his beer, left his money under his glass and left the bar without saying anything.

The woman thought she'd never see him again.

But the next night, he came back.

He waited for the woman who wore her dark hair in a beehive and talked like Loretta Lynn to finish her shift, and he took her out for a late-night dinner. They stayed out for a long time, talking about everything — their work, their days, their life, their pasts and their futures, until the restaurant finally locked the doors and turned out the lights and told them to go home.

My parents, before they were my parents, sat in my dad's car, talking and finding their voices deep into the night.

> Long after I should have been asleep, I remember overhearing my parents' late-night conversations.

You wonder what keeps a couple together for 40, 50, 60 years. You wonder what's the secret to a long and interesting marriage.

Once, I came across my parents' wedding photo, a single color print. They keep it in a photo box on a shelf, not even in a frame. In it, my mom is wearing a long, blue satin dress and white gloves; my dad is in a sharp, black suit. They're posed in front of a brown-paneled wall at the courthouse. They look happy. But they also look quiet. It doesn't seem right. That's the thing you notice when

you
stare at
pictures long
enough: They capture
everything but sound.

When I think of my parents,
I think first of their voices, the constants
that haven't changed despite age and
illness and surgeries and time. My dad's
hair isn't black anymore; my mother
doesn't wear a beehive. But their voices
are the same, as strong and distinct as
when I was young and would listen to
them talk at night.

When I was a child, long after I
should have been asleep, I remember
lying in bed, overhearing my parents'
late-night conversations.

They worked long hours back then
and got home well after suppertime.
They had a business to run and daily
things to take care of; every decision they
made was through careful conversation
with each other. Always with each other.

Every night, I listened to the
scrape of their forks on plates while
they ate their late-night dinner. And
I heard them talking. For hours at the
kitchen table, they talked — about
what I don't know, their pasts and
their futures, maybe? Their work, their
days, their life. Sometimes they raised
their voices; sometimes they argued.
But mostly, I heard my dad's hearty
laughter and my mom's sweet accent
sounding just like a country singer. And
I listened as their voices drifted up the
stairs in the night, finding their way
toward me, filling in the darkness.

To order more

If you've enjoyed *Wish You Were Here*, think of all your family, friends, and coworkers who would enjoy it, too!

CALL THE OUR STATE STORE
AT

(800) 948-1409

OR VISIT

OURSTATESTORE.COM

Our State
DOWN HOME IN NORTH CAROLINA